A Soul in Bondage

Stories from Tibet

Panda Books

Panda Books
First Edition 1992
Copyright 1992 by CHINESE LITERATURE PRESS
ISBN 7 – 5071 – 0087 – 1
ISBN 0 – 8351 – 2096 – 1

Published by CHINESE LITERATURE PRESS
Beijing 100037, China
Distributed by China International Book Trading Corporation
35 Chegongzhuang Xilu, Beijing 100044, China
P.O. Box 399, Beijing, China
Printed in the People's Republic of China

CONTENTS

Preface

Dondrup Wangbum

IN August 1991, I went to Lhasa to attend the Second International Symposium on Gesar Culture, and was met there by Tashi Dawa and Ma Lihua, poet and author of *Glimpses of Northern Tibet*. It was the second time I had met Tashi Dawa, the first time being exactly ten years before at a seminar on Tibetan literature. He was a very young man then and had just embarked on his literary career.

It was on the afternoon of August 14 in Ma Lihua's room that we had a rambling chat about almost everything under the sun. In the evening, I brought our conversation round to Tashi Dawa's literary works because I wanted to finish compiling *An Introduction to Contemporary Tibetan Literature* which I had started ten years before. Unfortunately, around ten o'clock, the electricity was cut off. Tashi Dawa went downstairs and brought back with him a lamp and we continued in its soft bright glow.

Tashi Dawa was born in Batang County in the Garze Tibetan Autonomous *Zhou* of Sichuan Province in 1959. His father was a government official. With the founding of the People's Republic of China, a large number of Tibetan people were sent to work in Tibet, and his father was one of them. Tashi Dawa spent most of his childhood in Chongqing, his mother's home. Like other children of government workers in Tibet, he frequently travelled from Chongqing to Nyingchi, or to Shigatse or Lhasa as his father was transferred from one place to another. After graduating from junior middle school in 1974, he studied painting at the exhibition centre of the Tibet Autonomous Region, and in the same year, became a stage designer at the local theatre. In 1978, he entered the Chinese Operatic Institute to follow a one-year advanced course in drama. His life in Chongqing and around the familiar Jialing River formed a solid basis for him to learn Chinese, which broadened his horizons and gave him greater scope to learn about other cultures around the world. It was with an open mind, therefore, that he "entered" Tibet, which, to him, was fresh and mysterious, and it is these qualities that are one of the main features of his works — the first of which was "Reticence" published in *Tibetan Literature* in 1979. It was this story that brought him to the attention of the Chinese literary world.

As a boy Tashi Dawa was imaginative and dreamy. He wanted to hear the wonderful music of the heavens resounding in the oppressive classroom. He hunched over his desk writing science-fiction, detective stories about his own heroism, putting all the weird ideas a junior middle school student could possibly have into his work. Sometimes, he would read with his friends or discuss international events. Reading is Tashi Dawa's favourite pastime. His early reading matter included mainly modern and contemporary Han Chinese literature and translated versions of Russian literature. In 1980 he developed an interest in American and Latin-American literature, including the works of J. L. Borges, Gabriel Garcia Marquez, J. J. Rulfo, Ernest Hemingway and William Faulkner. His early works, "Reticence", "Pilgrims" and "Over the River", for example, are simple and realistic. His work "White Poplar, Garland and Dream" describes the workings of the subconscious. "A Soul in Bondage" and "Tibet: the Mysterious Years" are written in a style best described as "magical realism". The publication of "A Soul in Bondage" has generated great interest in many circles. Those who study Latin-American literature will immediately recognize the Latin-American influence. His so-called trilogy of illusions, "The Glory of the Wind and Horse", "Invitation of a Century" and "The Light on the Cliff" is written in a more sustained, detailed way and delves into the heart of Tibetan society. The tragic overtones are immensely moving. Opinions about the trilogy differ, some critics acclaiming it and others denouncing it as unintelligible. Whatever one's opinion, however, it is undoubtedly a courageous work, and is of historical value not only to Chinese literature but even more so to Tibetan literature. I once told a Tibetan writer, "Read Tashi Dawa's works. It's true that he is deficient in some aspects, but his artistic methods and the questions he raises are valuable. No artist will succeed without incorporating others' strong points." He read some and told me he was inspired.

In China, quite possibly in other countries as well, the reason for being a writer is to express thoughts and emotions which reflect one's own rugged life. Tashi Dawa has gone through periods of depression, when he felt lost and hopeless, but he did not despair. On the contrary he thought hard, explored actively and found a way out for himself. He chose writing as his career — a hard but glorious one.

Tashi Dawa's works cover a wide range of subjects. His early works deal mostly with Lhasa, the capital of Tibet. He describes its people, its local events, its famous and prosperous Bajiao Street located in the city's centre, Jokhang Temple, the sweet-tea houses and the wine stalls. His later works explore a wider range of subjects and characters, such as the modern young man, Luozhu, in the story "Plateau Serenade", who wears sunglasses made in Italy, genuine jeans and long hair. This was the story that brought him fame. Still later he introduces two more characters. One is the veteran Agebu in "The Night Without Stars", and the other is the serf Langqin in "The Old Manor". The variety of his subjects truly reflects present-day Tibetan society from all perspectives.

History and reality, the new and the old — Tashi Dawa persistently sets himself between these and presents his readers with a changing, kaleidoscopic world. Although his descriptive methods vary, his themes are similar, even the same, as in "Balsang and His Sisters", "Invitation of a Century", and "The Old Manor".

In "Invitation of a Century", Tashi Dawa describes, through the use of illusion, an absurd yet thought-provoking story about two friends, Sangyi and Gyayang. The latter eventually becomes a young aristocrat of the past and shrinks from an adult to a foetus:

"When Sangyi caught sight of the girl with the

black mole on her chin, he could not believe his eyes.
She was still as young as ever, the only young girl in
the whole village now.

She stood silently, then went to the stables, while
the others gaped. She bent down to look at the
tiny creature, then lifted her skirt and a leg courageously, squatted, and sucked the foetus inside
her."

The river of time flows backwards and the life of
Gyayang returns to its original form. Because he is
Gyayang's friend, Sangyi becomes his scapegoat and
is thrown into prison. All these events show that the
old ways in Tibet still exert a powerful influence.

"The Old Manor" is clearer in meaning than
"Invitation of a Century". The male and female protagonists, like the battered and dilapidated manor, do
not rebuild themselves to meet the needs of new circum-
stances, but retain in their minds outmoded thoughts
until, years later, they eventually leave the new world.

The beautiful and cruel Lhamo Quzhen, owner of
the manor, in the past tortured the young and handsome Langqin, then her slave. Times change. After Liberation Langqin is transformed from being a serf to
being the leader of the cooperative team, director of the
poor peasants' association and chairman of the people's commune while Lhamo Quzhen lives in poverty
in a low hut, and becomes a plaything in the palm of
Langqin's hand. The "cultural revolution" sets them
both on the same level. At the end of the story he dies
a lonely death, she is on the point of death and the
manor has collapsed.

From his stories, firstly it may be clearly observed

that Tashi Dawa has put his finger on the pulse of Tibetan society, where religion and science, the new and the old, and the advanced and the backward co-exist. Like shelves displaying goods, his novels exhibit the old and the new together. Beneath the superficial peaceful atmosphere people undergo drastic psychological conflicts. The withdrawal of old ideas from the historical stage is evidently reluctant, and the new lack glamour and strength. What is clearly expressed here is the fact that the world is changing.

Secondly, traditional theories and the concept of typicalization are hardly appropriate tools for an evaluation of Tashi Dawa's works. As he says, "I'm a writer of feeling." "Feeling" is the pertinent word here for it reveals the origins of the themes and his descriptive methods. Feelings are changeable and always fresh. A single feeling may be trivial, but the combination of many feelings creates a colourful, imaginative world. It is the specific realistic environment of the Tibet in which Tashi Dawa lives that has aroused these various feelings and which are also the reason why he has neither conformed to conventional patterns nor repeated himself.

An important feature of Tashi Dawa's works is that he emphasizes Tibetan life in the '80s, and deals mostly with Tibetan youth. He articulates their thoughts and the conflicts raised by the tension between the demands of modernization and traditional culture, new and old values. This is commendably adventurous, and is not something often touched on by other Tibetan writers. His success is perhaps also due to the following:

First, he sharply contrasts modern civilization — the

outside world — with the reality of life in Tibet, a technique which leaves a deep impression on readers who do not know this part of the world.

Secondly, Tashi Dawa does not stop at describing local customs, but consciously or unconsciously, observes people's lives with the objective perspective of an outsider. Most Tibetan writers are too close, too familiar with the Tibetan life-style to be inspired by it.

Thirdly, Tibet is often called "mysterious Tibet". The interest of many readers, both at home and abroad, anxious to hear some weird, mysterious or fantastic story, is aroused as soon as Tibet is mentioned. Actually, the "mystery" of Tibet is the "mystery" of Tibetan culture, and this mystery stems from ignorance. Once it is understood, it is no longer mysterious. A Tibetan never thinks of himself or his life as a mystery; Tashi Dawa's "magical realism" satisfies people's desire to know Tibet, and the strange descriptions arouse empathy.

Tashi Dawa is a full-time writer, vice-chairman of the Writers' Association of the Tibetan Autonomous Region, an editor of *Tibetan Literature*, and a member of the Chinese Writers' Association. He has published two collections of short stories, *A Soul in Bondage* and *Invitation of a Century*. He is still young and has a bright future ahead of him. He has confidence in his literary talents and is at present working on a novel.

A Soul in Bondage

THERE is a Peruvian folk-song called *El Condor Pasa* that I have not heard for a long time. But its simple, yet solemn melody lingers in the mind. Whenever I hear it, it conjures up a vision of high plateaux and deep valleys; of bits of farm land carved out of hillsides; of straggly crops; mill houses beside streams, and low stone cottages; of mountain folk struggling under heavy loads, the sound of cow bells, and the lonely dust-devils whirling in the wind, under a dazzling sun.

My visions are not of Peru and the foothills of the high Andes. They are visions of the Pabunaigang Mountains in the south of Tibet. I am not sure whether I have actually been there, or merely dreamt of those mountains. I cannot be sure, for I have been to too many places to keep reality and fantasy separate. I realize now that, until I finally went there, the Pabunaigang Mountains in my mind were only the reflection of a 19th century landscape by Constable.

Although it was still a quiet mountain area, the lives of the people had quietly slipped into the modern era. There was a small airport, from which a helicopter made the trip into the city five times a week.

Nearby was a electric generator powered by solar energy. In a small restaurant next to the petrol station at Zhelu Village, I sat with a man with a beard. He was

a talker who went on and on. He was actually quite
well known, the chairman of the Himalayan Transportation Company; the only outfit in Tibet that owned
container trucks built in West Germany. I went to a
carpet factory where designers worked out their ideas
on computers. A satellite disc picked up five channels
and broadcast thirty-eight hours of programmes a day.

In spite of the material progress that has been made,
some of the old traditions live on among the people of
Pabunaigang Mountains. For instance, the village chief
who has a doctorate in agriculture still makes the curious ''lo-lo'' sound with his tongue when he speaks
to me as an expression of respect. And when people
ask a favour they still say, ''gu-ji, gu-ji'' in a
plaintive voice. Old men remove their hats and press
them to their breasts as a sign of respect. Although
weights and measures were standardized ages ago, people here still measure lengths by holding out one arm
and indicating the length they mean by chopping at it
with the palm of the other hand, from the wrist upwards, all the way to the shoulder.

Sangje Dapo, the living Buddha, was dying. He was
the twenty-third incarnation of the Buddha at Zatuo
Monastery. He was ninety-eight years old, and after
him there would be no successor. Sangje Dapo and I
had been friends. I had come to write an article about
him. When a religion as mysterious and as steeped in
legend such as Lamaism fails to produce a successor to
its many petty leaders, it declines. Those were my senti-
ments. Sangje Dapo thought otherwise. He shook his
head at me, and his eyes took on a faraway look.
''Sangbala,'' he said slowly, ''the battle of Sangbala
has begun.''

According to legend there is a paradise on earth to the north — the kingdom of Sangbala. It is said that the secret sect of the Yoga began there. The first king, Suocha Denapu was a disciple of Buddha, and later, went about preaching his message. Scriptures prophesy that one day, the kingdom of Sangbala will be invaded by a great host. "You will ride on, never turning back. Twelve divisions will follow you. You will aim your spear at the heart of Halu Taimeng, chief of demons and arch-enemy of Sangbala. And the demons will be routed." This was the anthem of the last king of Sangbala. Sangje Dapo had touched on the battle of Sangbala once before. He said the battle of Sangbala would go on hundreds of years, but the demons would be vanquished in the end. Then the tomb of Zunggeba would open, and once more the message of the Buddha would be preached. This would continue a thousand years, and then great winds and fire would sweep the earth. Finally, a deluge would bring about the end of the world, but a handful of souls would be spared. The world would begin again, with religion revived. Sangje Dapo lay in his cot, his eyes fixed on someone that only he could see, and it was this unseen presence that he addressed when he spoke: "When you've crossed the Kalong Glacier you will be standing in the palm of the Lord of the Lotus. Ask nothing. Seek nothing. In prayer you will find inspiration, and inspiration will bring visions. You will see out of the crisscrossing lines of that palm, one line leads to earthly paradise."

I seemed to visualize in that instant how it might have been when the Lord of the Lotus ascended into heaven. I seemed to see a chariot driven by two angels whisking him away into the southern sky.

"Two young people from Kangba are searching for the way to Sangbala," said the living Buddha.

"You mean to tell me, in the year 1988, a man and a woman...." I asked wearily.

He nodded.

"And the man was wounded?" I asked.

"Then you know the story," replied the living Buddha.

Sangje Dapo, the living Buddha, began to recall the story of the young man and woman who had come to Pabunaigang Mountains, and the things they had encountered on the way. As the story unfolded, I realized that I was listening to a tale I had written some time ago, and locked away in a trunk, without showing to anyone. Yet he seemed to be reciting the story, word for word. The place was a village named A on the road to Pabunaigang. The time was 1984. There were only two characters: a young man and a young woman. The reason I never showed the manuscript to anyone was because I did not know how to end the story. Listening to the living Buddha tell it made everything clear. The only difference was that at the end of my story the young man meets an old man in a tavern, and it is the old man who tells him where he must go. I did not describe the way ahead. I could not, because I did not know it at the time. Yet the living Buddha claimed that it was he who showed the two young people the road they must travel. There was yet another coincidence: both the old man in the story and the living Buddha spoke of the lines in the palm of the hand of the Lord of the Lotus.

Others drifted into the room, and gathered round

the cot. The living Buddha's eyes glazed, and gradually he slipped away.

The funeral preparations began. There were those who wanted to bury him in a stupa so that there would be a lasting monument. But Sangje Dapo was cremated. I left there shortly afterwards, musing on the source of inspiration in creative writing.

When I reached home, I opened a trunk labelled "Precious Rubbish". In it were all the manuscripts that had been rejected, and some that I did not wish published, all in neat brown paper envelopes. I found an envelope marked "840720" which contained an untitled short story. This is the story:

Jade first saw the man as she drove her sheep down the mountain. From where she stood he was no larger than a black speck moving slowly across the pebbly bottom of the dry riverbed. She could tell it was a man and that he would be coming towards her hut. She cracked her whip, and drove the sheep quickly down the incline.

It would be dark before the man got there, thought Jade. A few low huts built of stones from the riverbed stood on a small knoll. Behind were pens for the sheep. It was a desolate place. Two families lived here: Jade and her father, and a mute woman of about fifty who lived next door.

Jade's father was a story-teller and a singer. People came from all around to hire him. He had even been invited to perform in the cities. At times he would be gone a few days, but he was also known to stay away for months on end. When they came for him, they would usually bring an extra horse. And he would ride off with them, his six-stringed zither strapped to his back. The horses picked their way down the mountain gingerly, their copper saddle bells jingling and echoing through the wilderness. Jade would watch him go from the top of the knoll until the horses rounded a bend and were out of sight, stroking the big black dog that stood close to her.

It seemed that all her life was marked by the mingled sound of hoof beats and saddle bells. When she sat high on the mountain tending her flock, in her lonely daydreaming, she seemed to hear music rising out of the valleys, a wordless song of the spheres full of the irrepressible life of the wilderness, loneliness and yearning.

The mute woman who wove all day, clambered on to the knoll every morning at dawn, threw a handful of barley in the air, and cried out soundlessly to the Goddess of Mercy. Then, taking up her greasy prayer wheel, she faced the east and prayed. Now and then, Jade's father would steal into the woman's house in the dead of night, and tiptoe back to his own bed at the break of day wrapped in his long, shabby robe. Jade milked the goats, wolfed down a bowl of gruel, put up a bundle of food, picked up her soot-blackened pot, and drove the flock up the mountain. That was life.

Jade prepared some food and made the tea. Then she sprawled on the bed to wait. When the dog started barking, she rushed outside. It was already dark. At first she could see nothing. Then suddenly he stepped out of the darkness.

"It's all right; the dog won't hurt you," said Jade.

He was a tall, handsome young man. A red tassel

pinned to one side of his wide-brimmed hat trailed
past one temple.

Jade led the young man into her hut, and put food
before him. Her father was away, and the mute
woman's loom was the only sound that broke the silence. The young man was weary. After he had eaten
and thanked the girl, he threw himself on the father's
bed, and was fast asleep.

Jade stood on the threshold for a moment. The sky
was filled with stars, and the silence of the night envel-
oped her. The moonlight threw the peaks and the valleys into sharp relief. The big, black dog moved about
in a restless circle, straining on its tether. Jade
crouched beside it, and drew it close. She thought of herself, of this lonely place where she had changed from a
child into a young woman. She thought of her father
too, and of all the grim and silent men who came for
him. And she thought of the young stranger sleeping
in the hut, who came from a distant place, and would
be gone again in the morning. She wept. She knelt on
on the ground and hid her face, and prayed for her
father's forgiveness. She wiped her face on the dog's
neck, and went back into the hut. For a moment she
stood uncertainly in the dark, trembling in every limb.
Then silently she slipped under the sheep pelt beside
the young man.

When the morning star rose in the east, Jade rolled
up her thin blanket, and in the flickering light of the
oil lamp, stuffed strips of dried beef, a bag of barley,
some salt and a piece of yak butter into a sack. Then
she hung the little blackened cooking pot on her back.
She had all the things that a young girl ought to have
when she leaves home.

"I'm ready," she said.

The young man took another pinch of snuff, dusted the last particles from his hands and got to his feet. He rubbed the top of her head, put an arm about her shoulders and guided her out of the hut and turned westward where it was still dark. Jade carried everything on her back. She never even thought to ask where the young man would take her. Her only thought was that she was finally leaving this lonely, lifeless place. The young man carried a string of camphor wood prayer beads. It was all he owned. He walked erect, his head held high, filled with an unshakable faith in the long journey ahead.

"Why do you wear a leather thong round your waist? You look like a dog on a leash," he said.

"It's for counting the days," Jade replied. "See. There are five knots. That means we've been away from home five days."

"What's five days? I've never had a home."

She followed Tabei. They spent the nights on threshing floors, or in sheep pens. Sometimes they slept among the ruins of abandoned temples, or in caves. When they were lucky, they slept in a farmer's hut or in a shepherd's tent.

Whenever they came to a temple, they would kneel before each altar and touch their foreheads to the ground. Whenever they encountered a Manni cone they would find a few white pebbles to put on the top. There were many pilgrims along the way, slithering along on the ground. The heavy canvas aprons they wore were worn through at the chest and the knees, and patched over and over. Their faces were covered with grime, and on their foreheads were great black bruises from repeated knockings on the ground. The pieces of wood with nails hammered through them, which pilgrims used to pull themselves forward, left two deep furrows in the ground as they passed. Tabei and Jade walked and soon left the pilgrims behind.

The mountains of the Tibetan Plateau stretched into infinity. There were few people. They travelled for days at a stretch without seeing another soul or a village. They were battered by the cold blasts that blew out of the valleys, and the blazing sun scorched the earth. If one stood still and gazed up at the sky long enough, one would feel the earth shift under foot, as though one were in danger of being tossed into space. The mountains were wrapped in eternal silence. Tabei walked quickly, his lithe body held stiffly erect. Jade, carrying a heavy load on her back, gradually fell back. Tabei climbed on to a high rock and sat down to wait. They seldom spoke. When the silence became too much to bear, Jade would sing. It was a crude, tuneless sound that she made, more like an animal bellowing in distress than singing. Tabei would give her an impatient look, and she would fall silent again. Jade followed Tabei doggedly, speaking only when they stopped to rest.

"Is the wound still bleeding?"

"It's all right. It doesn't hurt anymore."

"Let me look at it."

"Catch me some spiders. I'll mash them and rub them on the wound. It will heal quicker."

"There aren't any spiders here."

"If you look in the cracks between the rocks you'll find some."

Jade dug up a few rocks that were half buried in

earth. She searched diligently, and in a little while caught five or six spiders. Tabei mashed them between the palms of his hands and rubbed the sticky substance on the wound on his calf.

"That dog was vicious. I kept running and the pot on my back was banging the back of my head so hard that I felt my eyes were popping out."

"I should have killed the dog!"

"The woman gave us one of these." Jade made a lewd sign with her hands.

Tabei scooped up some earth and sprinkled it on the wound, letting it dry in the sun.

"Where did she keep her money?"

"In the cupboard behind the counter. She had a wad like this," he held up two fingers to show her the size of the wad. "But I only took about ten notes."

"What are you going to buy?"

"There's a monastery at the foot of the mountain. I'm taking it to the Buddha, and keeping a bit for myself."

"Do you feel better now?"

"I feel fine, but I'm so thirsty I could die."

"I'll fetch some kindling."

Tabei stretched out on the rock and pulled his wide-brimmed hat over his eyes, chewing on a stalk of grass. Jade knelt in front of the fireplace built of stones, blowing on the smoldering kindling. The wood caught, sending out a spray of sparks. Jade scrambled to her feet, rubbing the smoke out of her eyes. A lock of hair on her forehead was singed.

Two shadowy figures appeared on a distant peak. They were probably shepherds tending their flocks, sitting there like a pair of vultures. Jade raised her right hand and waved. The distant figures waved back. They were so far away that a shouted greeting would not be heard.

"I thought we were the only people here," said Jade to Tabei.

"I'm waiting for the tea," Tabei replied shortly.

Jade suddenly remembered something. She took a booklet out of her robes and gave it to Tabei. She had lifted it out of the back pocket of a youth she had met in a village the night before, who had made advances. Tabei flipped through the booklet. He did not understand the drawings, nor could he read the text. On the cover was a picture of a tractor.

"It's useless," he pronounced and flung it back at Jade. Jade was crestfallen. It seemed she could do nothing right. Thereafter she used the pages to light fires for tea.

At dusk they saw a village at the foot of the mountain half hidden by trees. Jade's mood lightened. She sang, and taking up her staff did a wild dance, poking Tabei in the armpits and below the waist, trying to make him laugh. But Tabei seized the end of the staff and flung it aside with such force that it sent Jade sprawling in the dust.

They went on in silence. Once they reached the village, Tabei went off alone to drink in the tavern. They had agreed to meet later at the new school building where they would spend the night. The school was not yet completed and there were still no windows or doors, only openings. A film was being shown in the village square, and someone was hanging a screen on wooden poles. Jade went into a clump of trees to gather firewood. Suddenly she was surrounded by a swarm of children who threw stones at her. She tried to take no notice, though she was hit on the shoulder. It was not until a young man wearing a yellow cap came along that they ran off hooting and yelling.

"They threw eight stones at you and one hit you," smiled Yellow Cap. He had a pocket calculator in his hand which he showed to Jade. The numeral eight flashed on the screen.

"Where are you from?"

Jade looked at him dumbly.

"How long have you been travelling?"

"I don't remember," replied Jade. Then she showed him her leather thong. "Help me count."

"Does each knot represent a day?" He knelt beside her and counted ninety-two. "That's very interesting...."

"Really?"

"Didn't you count them yourself?"

Jade shook her head.

"Ninety-two days. Let's say you travelled twenty kilometres a day," he tapped the keys of his calculator. "That makes one thousand eight hundred and forty kilometres."

Jade did not understand numbers.

"I'm an accountant," the young man volunteered. "This thing helps solve all my problems."

"What is it?" asked Jade.

"It's a calculator. It knows everything. For instance it can tell me how old you are." He pressed some buttons, and showed the flashing figure to Jade.

"What does it mean?"

"It says you're nineteen."

"Am I really nineteen?"

"You tell me."

"But I don't know."

"Tibetans didn't used to keep track of their ages. But this knows, and it says you're nineteen."

"I don't think it's right."

"Let me look again. Maybe I misread it. I'm not quite used to the numbers yet."

"Does it know my name?"

"Of course."

"What is it then?"

He pressed some keys and filled the screen with figures.

"See? What did I tell you; it knows."

"What is it?"

"Don't you know yourself? You're really ignorant."

"How do you read it?"

"You read it like this," he help up the calculator for Jade.

"Do all those little flashing things say 'Jade'?"

"Of course it says 'Jade'."

Jade giggled delightedly.

"That's nothing. Foreigners have been using these for ages. I've been thinking about a problem. We work from day to night. According to economic theory the value of labour should equal the value of goods produced." He rambled on, throwing in bits of labour relations, the ratio between the value of labour and value of manufactured goods. He even mixed in something about the year, the month, the day, addition, subtraction, multiplication and division. It was a hodge-podge that made no sense. Finally a figure flashed on the calculator screen.

"Look at that! We end up with a debit. That means at the end of the year we have to go cap in hand to the state for supplies of grain…. That's against all the laws of economics! Well, what are you staring at?"

"I was thinking if you haven't any food, you could eat with us. I was just gathering firewood to cook the evening meal."

"Damn it, you must have come out of the dark ages. Or maybe you're from another planet?"

"I come from a faraway place…." she reached for her thong. "How many days did you say?"

"Eighty-five, I think."

"That's not right. You said ninety-two, you liar." Jade laughed.

"I think I'm drunk," he muttered shutting his eyes.

"Will you eat with us? I still have a bit of dried beef."

"Girl, why don't you come with me? I'll take you to a place where there are happy young people. There is music and beer and disco. Drop that bundle of twigs and come with me."

Tabei pushed his way out of the crowd watching the film. He had been drinking but he was not drunk. It was the coloured images, now large, now small, flitting across the screen that made his head ache. He stumbled into the unfinished building. Jade's little black pot was perched on a pile of stones, and her things were stowed in a corner. Tabei felt the hearth stones. They were cold. He gulped a mouthful of cold water and leaned against the wall, deep in thought. The villages ahead would lose their original tranquillity more and more; they would become noisy and clamorous. There would be the roar of machines, laughter, music, voices raised in joy and anger. He wanted none of those things. He wanted to be rid of the confused sounds of humanity. He was seeking something quite different.

Jade finally stumbled into their camp. She leaned heavily against the wall, and even at that distance she reeked of liquor. But Tabei could tell she had been drinking something better than he had.

"They are so happy," she gurgled between laughter and tears. "They are as happy as the gods.... Let's not leave the day after tomorrow.... Let's stay a day longer...."

"No," he said. Tabei never stayed more than one night in a place.

"I'm weary. I'm so very tired." Jade shook her head.

"You don't know what it is to be weary. You have the legs of a cow. You're never tired."

"You don't understand," she protested. "It's not the body that I'm talking about."

"You're drunk. Got to sleep." He dragged her down, and pressed her onto the ground. Afterwards he made another knot on her leather thong.

Jade was weary. Every time she lay down to rest, she felt she could not get up again. She did not want to go on.

"Get up. Don't lie there like a lazy bitch," Tabei ordered.

"I don't want to go on," Jade lay in a patch of sunlight, gazing up at him through half-opened lids.

"What did you say?"

"You go on alone. I don't want to follow you day after day. You don't know where you're going. You'll wander for ever."

"Women don't understand anything." He knew where he was going.

"Maybe I don't understand," she shut her eyes again.

"Get up!" He kicked her in the rump, and raised his hand to strike her. "Get up or I'll beat you!"

"You're a devil!" cried Jade, scrambling to her feet. Tabei turned and walked away, leaving Jade to scramble after him as best she could.

One night, Jade ran away. She strapped the little pot on her back and stole away into the night. She picked her way down the mountain by the light of the moon and stars. The next day, as she rested beside a deep chasm, she saw a figure approaching from a distance. It was as it had been the first time she saw Tabei. He caught up with her and she turned on him with the ferocity of a cornered beast. She seized the pot and smashed at him with all her might. But the blow went wide. He knocked the pot from her grasp and sent it bouncing into the chasm. They heard it rattling down to the bottom. She climbed down the chasm after it. It was hours before she pulled herself up again. The little pot was full of dents.

"Look what you've done to my pot," wailed Jade.

Tabei took the pot from her, and they examined it together.

"There's only one small crack," he remarked. "I'll fix it."

Tabei turned away, and Jade followed reluctantly.

Suddenly she threw back her head and sang, and her strange, wild song echoed from peak to peak and down into the valleys.

The truth was Tabei was weary of Jade. He believed that in a past life he had accumulated enough merit to have escaped the underworld and been reborn. But on his way to Nirvana woman and gold were the stumbling blocks that he must rid himself of.

Soon after they came to a village called A. By that time the leather thong around Jade's waist was a mass of tight little knots. The villagers came out to greet them with drums and gongs. The militia formed a guard of honour, holding up semi-automatic rifles with red rags stuffed in the muzzles for safety's sake. Four villagers dressed as cows danced in the road. The village chief and some young girls came forth to greet them carrying *hadas* whose spouts had been smeared with yak butter. There had been a drought in the village. A soothsayer had prophesied that a couple would come from the east that day, and they would bring rain. At dusk when Tabei and Jade appeared, the villagers believed them to be the two people they were expecting. So they came out to meet the strangers in their festive garb. Tabei and Jade were hustled onto a tractor and driven into the village. The houses in the village were decorated in coloured prayer flags. Many of the onlookers thought they recognized the traits of the Goddess of Mercy in the way Jade spoke and carried herself. To them she was the manifestation of the Goddess. For the first time Tabei was totally ignored. However, Tabei knew Jade was not a manifestation of a divine being. He had watched her in her sleep, and had come to loathe her ugliness, for her face grew slack and saliva dribbled from her half-opened mouth.

Tabei went to a tavern bent on getting drunk and picking a fight. If he annoyed someone enough to pull a knife, so much the better.

There was only an old man drinking in the tavern. Tabei sat down insolently across from him. A village wench with a coloured kerchief tied around her head put a glass before him and poured the wine.

Tabei quaffed the wine, slammed the glass down and cried out, "This wine is like horse's piss."

No one took any notice.

"Do you think it's horse's piss?" Tabei asked the old man.

"I drank horse's piss once when I was young. Right out of the thing dangling between a stallion's legs."

Tabei chuckled.

"I was trying to get my herd back from the bandit Amelia. I followed her all the way from Geze to the Takalamagan desert."

"Who was this Amelia?"

"That was a decade ago. Amelia was a bandit queen, a Kazak who came from Xinjiang. She was a terror in Ali and the north of Tibet. She would sweep down on a herd under the cover of night, and in the morning all that was left were jumble of hoof prints. Even the government troops couldn't stop her."

"Then what happened?"

"Well, I took my gun, got on my horse and chased her into the desert. And a few mouthfuls of horse's piss saved my life."

"What happened then?"

"The bandit queen wanted to keep me as her...."

"Husband?"

"As her goat herder. And I was the owner of a herd of ten thousand! But she was beautiful, as dazzling as the sun, and no one dared look at her. In the end I escaped. To tell you the truth, aside from heaven and hell I've been everywhere."

"But you haven't been where I'm going," said Tabei.

"Where is that?" asked the old man.

"I'm not sure." For the first time Tabei was uncertain of the way ahead. The old man seemed to understand.

The old man pointed to the mountain behind him and said, "Nobody's been there. This village used to be a post station once. There was nowhere you couldn't reach from here, but nobody has been in those mountains. Back in 1964," he went on dreamily, "the communes were just beginning. Everybody was talking about communism, but nobody knew what it was. They said it was some kind of paradise, but nobody knew where it was. The Tibetans didn't know where it was. Neither did the Alis, nor those from Qinghai. But no one had been across the Kalong Glacier so it had to be there. A few people sold all they had and went off to find communism. They never came back. No one cared to follow them, no matter how hard things got."

Tabei gripped the rim of his glass between his teeth and gazed at the old man thoughtfully.

"But I know a secret that lies at the foot of the Kalong Glacier," added the old man.

"Tell me."

"Are you prepared to go there?"

"Maybe."

"When you reach the top of the mountain, you will hear a weeping sound. It sobs like an abandoned child. But it's only the wind blowing through a crevice. It will take you seven days to reach the top. It will be sunrise. Rest. Don't be in a hurry to descend. The light reflected off the snow will blind you. Wait till dark, then begin your descent."

"That's no secret," said Tabei.

"That's not the secret. Two days after you have crossed to the other side of the mountain, you will come to a plain crisscrossed by a thousand creeks and gullies that seem to run in all directions. It's like a maze. That's not a secret either, but don't interrupt. Do you know where those creeks and gullies come from? They are the lines on the right palm of the Lord of the Lotus. Aeons ago, the Lord of the Lotus battled a demon called Shibameriru. They fought for one hundred and eight days, and though the Lord of the Lotus used all his magical powers he could not vanquish the demon. Finally, the demon turned himself into a flea, that he might evade the Lord. But the Lord stretched out his hand and smashed the flea straight into hell. The force of that blow left the print of his right palm on the earth. It is said that humans who enter that maze will be lost for ever. However, there is one route out. But there are no markings on it whatsoever."

Tabei stared at the old man solemnly.

"That is only a legend, I don't really know whether it's true," muttered the old man.

Tabei made up his mind to go there. The old man came to him then and proposed that he leave Jade be-

hind for his son. The son had recently bought a tractor. These days every family wanted one. In the morn-
ings, the rumbling of the tractors drowned out the
crowing of the roosters. And while they drank the
cool, clear water of the mountain streams, they smelt
the faintly pungent odour of petrol. The old man oper-
ated a mill powered by electricity, and his wife farmed
ten *mu* of land. Not long ago he had attended a meeting of farmers who had prospered, and received an
award. His picture was in the newspapers. No generation in their family had been as prosperous or as busy
as they. Now they needed a sensible woman to take
charge of the household, and a wife for his son. While
they were still talking the son came in. He flashed a
wad of notes in front of the stranger. He wore a wrist-
watch, and a walkman was strapped to his waist.
Earphones were stuck to his ears. He danced to music
that no one else could hear. He was the epitome of the
young man of the city. Tabei was not impressed. What
interested him was the tractor parked outside. The engine had not been switched off, and the tractor emitted
a put-put sound. Tabei ran his fingers over the steering-
wheel enviously.

"I'll leave Jade for you," said Tabei. From the
way he smiled, Tabei knew the young man had probably already had Jade.

"Can I drive this contraption?" asked Tabei.

"Of course. You can learn to drive it in half an
hour," the young man said expansively. He quickly
showed Tabei how to control the machine, how to reg-
ulate the accelerator, shift the gears, and how to start
and stop.

Tabei drove the tractor along the dirt path in the

gathering dusk. Jade watched from the side of the
road, her eyes brimming with joy, for she was going to
stay. Just then a heavier tractor towing a load came
careening down the path. The driver saw Tabei in front
of him but it was too late to stop. Tabei panicked, not
knowing what to do. The young man shouted for him
to drive the tractor into the ditch by the side of path.
At the last moment, Tabei leaped from the driver's
seat. The tractor slid into the ditch, but the oncoming
tractor caught Tabei and knocked him to the ground.
Everyone rushed to him. Tabei picked himself up. He
had been struck in the side, but to everyone's relief,
aside from a good dusting, he was none the worse for
wear.

Tabei was leaving. He took Jade in his arms and
touched his forehead against hers, and went off
towards the Kalong Glacier. That evening it rained,
and the whole village celebrated. On the way Tabei
began to spit blood.

The manuscript ended there.

I decided to return to Papunaigang, and cross the
Kalong Glacier to the place they called the palm print
of the Lord of the Lotus. Perhaps I would encounter
my protagonist again.

The distance from A Village to the Kalong Glacier
was farther than I imagined. The mule I hired went
lame. It lay on the ground, white froth dribbling from
its mouth, its eyes rolled back in the throes of death. I
unstrapped the saddlebags, and shouldered them myself, and leaving a handful of meal beside the mule's
muzzle, went on my way. At the top of the mountain
the wind roared. Yet the air was calm but bitterly cold.
The snow lay in unbroken undulations for as far as

the eye could see.

I began the descent. I had goggles so I did not have to wait till dark. Slowly I zigzagged my way down. The saddlebags grew heavier and heavier, as they slipped down to the small of my back. I stopped to adjust them. As I leaned forward, the weight shifted, I lost my balance and pitched forward. I felt myself helplessly sliding down the mountainside. I drew myself into a tight ball, and tumbled head over heels down the mountain. When I came to I was lying at the foot of the mountain. A deep furrow marked my passage through the snow ending where snow and mist melted into one another. I had looked at the time when I was on the mountain top and distinctly remembered it was 9:46, yet now my watch registered 8:03. Beyond the snow line, the earth was covered with moss, and further down there was grass, which gave way to low brush and then short, stubby trees, and finally forest. Beyond the forest, the vegetation grew sparse again. Great boulders jutted out of the dry earth. I noticed all this while I had been checking the time, comparing what I thought it should be to what my watch registered. I concluded that somehow after I crossed the Kalong Glacier time began to move backwards. The calendar and the hands on my watch spun in reverse, five times faster than normal.

The landscape took on a dreamlike quality. There was row upon row of Bodhi trees with elliptical leaves and yellowish-white bark, and roots that were so neat they might have been deliberately carved. To one side there stood the ruins of an ancient monastery. Suddenly a huge elephant came lumbering towards me across the clearing. The landscape took on the nightmarish

quality of Salvador Dali's *Temptation of St. Anthony*.
I hastened to put some distance between myself
and the beast, and did not stop till I reached the
banks of the hot springs. I was exhausted but I dared
not sleep for fear that I might never wake again. Beyond the hot springs the plain was littered with gold
saddles, bows and arrows, rusted spears, armour, scrip-
ture cases and tattered banners. It appeared to be an
ancient battlefield out of some forgotten epic. If I was
not so tired I would have ventured forth for a closer
look. As it was I gazed at this curious spectacle from a
distance. Long exposure to the steam had melted the
metal, so that the various objects melded into indistinct
masses. I was beginning to wonder if I was seeing
things. Long isolation plays strange tricks on the
mind. But my reasoning and memory were unaffected.
The sun still rose from the east and set in the west.
Though night still followed day, the backward spinning of the dials on my watch was disconcerting. It
disturbed my metabolism, and shifted my centre of
gravity.

At dawn I woke under a huge red boulder. I found
myself at a point where a thousand creeks and gullies
fanned out in every direction. I had reached the palm
of the Lord of the Lotus. I clambered up the side of a
gully and looked over the rim. The empty plain swept
onto the horizon. Some of the gullies that crisscrossed
it were bottomless. The plain must have endured a
long drought, for the earth was cracked and scorched
to a cinder; not a blade of grass grew. It reminded me
of the final scene of a film I once saw. The earth was
emptied of life by a nuclear holocaust. Only a man
and a woman survived. They struggled painfully to-

wards each other, and embraced at the fade-out. They were the new Adam and Eve.

But my protagonist did not appear.

"Tabei ... Tabei ... Where are you?" I shouted. The sound travelled far but there was no echo. I felt he could not have found his way out of the maze.

A while later a figure appeared in the distance, moving slowly towards me. I ran to meet it, shouting Tabei's name at the top of my lungs. When I got closer, I found it was Jade.

"Tabei is dying," she sobbed.

"Where is he?"

Wordlessly she led me into a nearby ravine. Tabei lay at the bottom of the ravine. He was pale and wan, and his breathing came in short painful gasps. Moss covered the sides of the ravine, and water dripping from the cracks in the rock had collected into a small pool. Jade soaked her belt in it and squeezed the water into Tabei's half-open mouth.

"Master, I have been waiting. I comprehend and the gods will inspire me," Tabei said, lifting his eyes to me beseechingly.

"He has a serious wound in the side," Jade whispered to me. "He has to keep drinking water."

"Why didn't you stay in the village?" I asked.

"Why would I stay there?" she retorted. "I never considered staying. Besides, he would never let me go. He took my heart and tied it to his belt. I can't live without him."

"That's not so," I objected.

"He wants to know what that is?" Jade pointed in the direction from which I came. I looked back. Before me was a deep gully, as straight as an arrow. At the end of it was a huge red boulder. That was where I had spent the night. On the rock was carved the symbol of a bow. It was the pictorial representation of a sound Tibetans made when they had recited the six syllables of their chant a hundred times. I concluded the strange marking must either mean that this was a place which gods and demons frequented, or it marked the resting place of a dead hero. I had seen such a rock on the banks of the Quimixingu River commemorating the Tibetan hero Benlatin II who fought the British invaders in 1904. But I felt no need to explain all this to Tabei. It was too late to explain the truths I had discovered. I had given life and purpose to all my "children", who like Jade and Tabei were consigned to a serial numbered brown paper envelope. But I had made a grave error in their creation. I should have made them human beings of the new era. The act of creation is objective. How would I answer to letting characters like them wander the world in our time?

I crouched beside Tabei, pressed my lips close to his ear and tried to tell him in words that he could grasp that the place he sought all his life did not exist any more than Thomas More's *Utopia*.

But it was too late. In the last moments of life, nothing would shake his faith. He turned his body and pressed his head against the earth.

"Tabei," I said, "you will get better. I have some medicine in my saddlebags over there."

"Hush," Tabei pressed his ear hard against the moist damp earth. "Listen! Listen!"

I listened but all I could discern was the wild beating of my heart.

"Help me up there! I must get up there!" Tabei

pushed himself up to a sitting position, shouting and gesticulating.

I helped him to his feet. Jade climbed to the top of the ravine and I, holding Tabei round the waist with one arm and dragging myself forward with my free hand, gradually inched our way upward. It was a painfully slow climb. I gashed the palm of my hand on a sharp rock. At first it was numb, then a sharp pain shot down the length of my arm, and the blood trickled down the sleeve of my jacket. I hung on doggedly. Finally we were almost level with the edge of the ravine. Jade reached down and seized Tabei by the armpits, and I pushed from below and in this way half dragged and half lifted him over the edge. The sun was peeping over the horizon. Tabei dragged the air into his lungs in greedy gulps, looking round all the while as though he were searching for something.

"What are they saying, Master? I can't understand. Tell me please, I beg of you!" Tabei prostrated himself before me. Then Jade and I heard it too. It was a sound that came from the sky.

"It's temple bells," cried Jade.

"It's church bells," I corrected her.

"It's an avalanche!" said Jade.

"It's a thousand people singing," I corrected her again. Jade looked at me quizzically.

"The gods are speaking," said Tabei simply.

This time I did not attempt to correct him. How could I explain that the man's voice was speaking in English; that this was a live broadcast from the 23rd Olympics in Los Angeles that was beamed to every corner of the globe by a space satellite? Finally, the sense of time came back to me. The dials on my watch stopped all at once. It read: July 1984, 7:30 a.m. Beijing time.

"It's not the gods speaking, it's man's challenge to the world, my son," I said to him.

I didn't know whether he heard me, or if he understood. He curled up as if he were very cold, his eyes shut tightly as if asleep. I knelt beside him, and gently arranged his body in the shape of a bow. The blood of my injured hand stained his tattered clothes. I felt a pang. I had killed him, as surely as I had killed so many other protagonists. It's time I stopped.

"I'm all alone now," Jade said pathetically.

"Never mind. You've endured enough. I'll remould you."

I looked up at her, and she gazed back at me, full of innocence and trust.

The leather thong around her waist dangled before my eyes. I took hold of it and counted the knots that marked the days of her long trek. There were one hundred and eight, the same number as Tabei's string of prayer beads.

The sun had risen. I took Tabei's place and Jade followed behind. We were going back, but time was moving forward.

Translated by David Kwan

Tibet: the Mysterious Years

1910—1927

WHEN the twelve-year-old Dalang went round the back of the cottage to piss, a red-headed bird with blue wings alighted on the ground in front of him. Crouching, he pounced on it like a frog. The bird slipped through his fingers, and darted to a rock beyond reach. He moved forward and kept after it till he reached a little waterfall by a stream where the bird flew off. As he stood on the grassy ground looking down along the slope, he saw a man coming up towards Gokam. At first he was not sure the man was heading for Gokam, because, at the col of the mountain, the road branched off towards Bangdui Manor. Entering the valley, the man began to climb along the splashing brook. Dalang rushed back to the cottage and told everyone what he had seen.

All the villagers of Gokam came out and stood on the grass by the stream, watching the man's ascent. Two households with six people lived in Gokam: Wangme, his wife in her forties, with a big tumour hanging from her neck, his son Dalang and daughter Qionla; the other household consisted of an old couple, the seventy-five-year-old Mima and his faithful wife. With no children to help them, they clung to each other for survival. They stood there in silence, watching the stranger getting closer with each step. Every time Gokam was visited by outsiders, one or two families would be taken away. In five years, hardly any households remained.

After her parents died, a beautiful girl by the name of Logar, fell into the habit of singing. She sang when getting up in the morning, she sang when tending the sheep, she sang when angry, even the groans she made when she was ill sounded like songs. No matter what she was doing she would carelessly pull up her skirt and show her white legs, making the village men turn their eyes on her as if enamoured. Even Wangme, the father of two children, would sometimes sneak into her room at night when his wife was fast asleep. However, she was not going to marry anybody, because, as the villagers knew, she was waiting for somebody to take her away from the mountain.

One day when Logar was grazing her sheep on the hillside, an enormous man wrapped in black fur appeared suddenly and ate up all the food in Logar's room. When the villagers found him, he was lying asleep at the door. When they woke him up and asked where he had come from, he did not say a word but uttered unintelligible shrieks, his hands gesticulating madly. When they discovered that he was a retarded mute, they left, feeling bored. Logar bolted the door which she had seldom bolted before, and kept the man with her for the night. At midnight, they heard her screaming and all the men in the village picked up sticks, intending to rush out and punish the mute. After a moment, she stopped screaming and began singing again. Seeing there was no need to worry about her, they closed their doors and went back to

sleep. The next day someone discovered that the black
fur the man was seen wearing was not a coat but his
natural hair. As he sat in the sun, parting his hair to
look for lice, someone caught sight of his red navel.
Mima, who had been a huntsman when young, had
watched him carefully and told the villagers that he
was not a mute at all but a wild man-like creature that
had come out from the depths of the mountain.
Scared, the villagers hurried back and bolted their
doors from within, praying to Bodhisattva to protect
them. Logar was scared to death too but, as she had
become his prisoner, she had to go with him. That evening, after she had packed her clothes and provisions,
she went to say goodbye to the villagers who were hiding behind closed doors, and climbed onto the creature's back, humming songs with tears in her eyes.
Holding Logar tight to his back with one hand and
with the other hand crawling along the ground, the
creature leapt downhill. From his agile monkey-like
movements the villagers were convinced that he was a
wild man-creature. They pitied Logar for the sins she
had committed in her previous life. Being no match for
the powerful creature, the men gave vent to their frustration, swearing at the beast while trampling savagely
on the ground.

Before long a senior lama of the Red Sect came by
and announced that he was going to stay there in seclusion for three years and three months. No sooner had
he arrived than several households offered to wait
upon him at their homes. The lama took a look
round at the desolate scene to the north — a stream
flowing down from the top of the Drera Mountain;
to the east — precipitous, overhanging cliffs; to the

south — a mountain soaring from the valley up into the sky. Shaking his head, he said that a great master of the Esoteric Sect who had attained the Way was practising lamaism there and that it would disturb him if he stayed in the same place. So saying, he turned, about to go downhill. When the villagers tugged at his *kasaya* and asked him to explain further, he said those who were supposed to understand naturally understood, but to those who were not supposed to understand there was no need to explain. Right there and then, a few men who desired to become monks decided to go with the travelling lama as his disciples.

A few days later, there came another man, clad in rags, as unrestrained in his manner as a lunatic, muttering unintelligible incantations. He stayed in the home of the widow Gyayang Zholgar whose husband had just departed with the lama. On the third day the man took the widow away. Later it was rumoured that he was a friar of the Esoteric Sect and, in order to practise "resurrection of the dead", he had tortured Gyayang Zholgar to death in a variety of ways and used her corpse as the target of his practice. During the course of practice, the dead woman twice put out her tongue and twice he failed to catch it with his teeth. When the corpse put out her tongue the third time he managed to get it between his teeth but, as he was not well-practised, he was not able to bite the tip of her tongue off, instead, his own tongue, together with his windpipe and bowels, were yanked out by the corpse, and he dropped down dead on the spot. As a result, Gyayang Zholgar was resurrected. Wrapped in a snow-white woollen gown, she left the secret place where she had been kept and became a nun at a convent. Not long ago when Wangme crossed the mountain pass on his way to Xalung County, he made a special trip to visit her on behalf of the Gokam villagers and left offerings at the altar of the convent.

The man who had come to Gokam was a carpenter, called Cedoje. He lived at Bangdui Manor, about three or four hours' walk from Gokam. He had just come from Lhasa, claiming that he was Wangme's younger brother. He said his old mother had asked him to come and look for his brother. All that Wangme knew was that he had been abandoned as a child. He never knew that his mother had been living at Bangdui, nor did he know that he had ever had a brother. Sizing up the stranger, he shook his head suspiciously. Not until the bearded Cedoje had pulled him aside and told him that there was a coinsize red birth-mark on his thigh did he believe that he really was his younger brother. Besides, Wangme's careful wife observed that they had the same habit of slightly shrugging their right shoulders when they spoke and both had a slight squint in their eyes. That settled it.

The villagers gathered in Wangme's cottage, listening to the news Cedoje told about the outside world while drinking buttered tea out of bowls. In one corner there was a pot of mutton stew on the fire and its tempting aroma pervaded the whole room. Cedoje took the cow-horn snuff-bottle from Mima and put a pinch of snuff on his thumb nail. Blowing his nose, he slowly began to talk. It was a sad story. Less than three months after the Thirteenth Dalai Lama had returned to Lhasa after spending five years in exile, he was driven out to India by the warlord of Sichuan Province. Cedoje shook his head and so did his listeners. He also related all sorts of strange things he had heard on his way to Gokam. Finally he told how it had been his mother's wish that he came, as she did not have much time to live and she longed for the son she had become separated from forty years ago. She had not intended to abandon her son; she was on the run with refugees when in confusion, she had snatched up a conical willow basket, one of many and hurried on her way. The next day she discovered that she had been carrying turnips in her basket. But, ever since becoming a Buddhist, she had kept practising how to be virtuous, so Bodhisattva, to reward her, had revealed to her in a dream her son's whereabouts. That was how Cedoje had found Gokam — by following the instructions his mother had received in her dream. Besides, if the land she had rented on Bangdui Manor remained uncultivated for two years running, Degun Rinqin's manager would take it over and she would have to pay rent and do unpaid labour all the same.

There was silence in the room. The next day, when the sun rose from behind the mountain, only one household would be left in Gokam. Before Wangme's wife had time to spoon out the mutton from the pot, Mima stood up with difficulty and left with a heavy heart, his wife Caxun following him.

It was quiet in Gokam that night. Towards dawn, quietness reigned as if every noise in the universe had been engulfed by the Zela Mountain.

When Caxun woke up before daybreak, she had a funny feeling in her belly. Running her hand over it, she felt a lump as big as a fist. Surprised, she kicked at Mima who had just gone to sleep having tossed and turned on the thin mattress most of the night. He woke up and, putting out his hand to feel it, reassured her that she was pregnant.

"A fat chance!" Caxun said with a mixed expression on her face. "I never got pregnant when we were younger. How could it be possible with our hair turned conch-white and most of our pearl-like teeth fallen out?"

"This is where pregnancy occurs, near the spleen. It must be a girl." Mima was excited.

"How can you know more about women than women do?" Caxun was amazed.

Mima took no notice of her. Crouching against the wall and counting the white marks on it by the light of the lamp which was kept alight throughout the night, he said, "Today is a day of worship. Get ready quickly."

Caxun slipped into her clothes and set about making tea.

The first rays of the morning sun were obscured by the mountain ranges and the fading moonlight was still reflecting on the stream and the grass. Holding a pot of hot tea and a bagful of barley flour, Caxun opened the door, and was immediately confronted with a gust of fresh chill morning air. She carefully picked her way along the dimly visible path which was soon crossed by the stream. Unable to distinguish the stepping stones across it, she pulled up her skirt and waded through, her bare feet and legs assaulted by the cold water. She came to a huge precipitous rock and at the foot of the rock there was a hole as wide as a big earthenware pot. She squatted down, her face even with the hole. It was usually very difficult to find as it was covered with wild grass and tangled vines growing

from between the rocks. Parting the grass and vines
with her hands, Caxun brought out from the cave an
empty tea pot and an empty leather bag and then put
the pot of hot tea and the full bag of flour into the
cave. As the altar in the cave was covered with a piece
of thick cloth, when the pot and the bag were placed
on it there was no noise so the great master perfecting
himself in the cave was not disturbed. Finally she
pulled the grass and vines back over the cave, leaving
no trace of any disturbance. Moving backwards a few
steps, she knelt on the ground, kowtowing three times
and murmuring the "six-word mantra" with her palms
held together before her. By now there were people
moving about Wangme's cottage which was scarcely
visible in the whitish mist and smoke.

Cedoje woke up troubled by a sense of guilt over the
nightmare he had had the previous night. He was
ashamed to relate his dream to Wangme but, eventually after breakfast, he did so.

"Don't worry. I often have dreams like that. Sometimes I dream that I'm biting the pillar of the room. It
is a common dream in Gokam." Wangme did not
take it seriously. He was busy packing up for the journey to Bangdui.

Cedoje had dreamed that he was biting somebody's
plump leg. It seemed to be the leg of the mistress of
the tavern at Longzijia but it was also like the leg of
his sleepy aunt who had often visited his family when
he was small. This could be proof that this place had
once been haunted by hungry ghosts. No wonder so
many families had left Gokam, he thought.

Before Wangme's family and his brother departed a
little after noon, they each drank a bowl of light wine

they had saved from the pot. They dipped their ring
fingers into the wine three times and flicked them into
the air — a sign of blessing and a prayer for safety.
Wangme's wife wrapped every little thing into a large
parcel and carried it on her back, tear marks on her
face and eyes swollen, as if she had been crying bitterly. Cedoje carried a few worn wheat-straw mattresses
on his head, a small table in each hand; the daughter
was driving the dozen or so sheep. Wangme came out
last, holding the sleeping Dalang who was drunk with
the wine. He handed his son over to Mima, saying,
"This is our small way of saying 'Thank you'. Take
this child as a little dog to keep you company. It
won't be too much trouble to bring him up and he
can easily be fed on leftovers."

"Well...." Wangme had a strong sense of brother-
hood, offering his beloved son as a gift to his old
neighbour. Thinking of what his wife had just discovered, Mima had mixed feelings about taking the child.
But could he refuse point-blank by telling him that
soon they were going to have a child of their own?
Who would believe him, for his wife was an old
woman turning seventy?

Two hours had already passed before Wangme and
his family turned the corner of the mountain by a
patch of sand. All the way, they walked unsteadily like
drunkards. The mattresses on Cedoje's head had fallen
off. He stood by a waterfall, shouting to warn the
others to be careful. Wangme was just about to turn
his head and wave his hand when he tripped over a
rock and fell.

When Dalang woke up, he found himself lying in a
strange place, with an old couple gazing at him, their

wrinkled noses almost touching his cheeks.

"Where's my dad?" he asked.

The old couple straightened up and looked at each other, not knowing what to say.

"They've left me behind in Gokam, haven't they?" he wailed, and jumped up and ran out from under the old man's arm.

When Caxun was only two months pregnant Cering Gyamo was born. On the day she was born, a sweet shower fell all over the mountain areas. After the shower, a rainbow appeared in the distant sky which was a sign of good luck. On the fifth day, in the absence of neighbours and relatives, they observed the cleansing ceremony for the infant. They collected some pebbles and set them together in front of their cottage and using sweetgrass and pine twigs made a fire next to them. Putting a pinch of barley flour on the baby's forehead and coating her face and fluffy hair with glistening butter, they left the girl to bathe in the sunlight, while the old couple themselves sat against the wall, dozing off. After a while, Mima was awakened and as he opened his eyes he saw Dalang picking up the baby from the grassy ground and teasing her. Poking at her cheeks with his dirty black fingers, he said repeatedly, "When you grow up, you shall be my woman." When he saw that the old couple were looking at him coldly, he laid the baby on the ground and slunk off like a cat that had been found stealing food. Mima and his wife knew that, instead of trying to catch up with his family on their way to Bangdui, Dalang had settled somewhere nearby. They wondered how a boy of just over ten years old could manage to make a living when there was no sign of anybody else living there.

The next day after Wangme and his family had left, Mima opening his door in the morning, found that overnight Gokam had become a desolate place like a deserted village with ruins of houses and broken walls. In front of Wangme's door, cobwebs had been hanging for years. The door frame had cracks in it as if made of rotten wood that was scarcely able to prop up the adobe and earth above. Rats scurried in and out through the door and the window. The ungainly pheasants that inhabited the bushes and the deep ravine behind the Zela Mountain, trailing their long blue tails, had now flown here to Gokam. Swaggering around, they cooed to each other and picked at food among the deserted ruins. A few grey and light-brown rabbits jumped out from the hillside and sat up in vigilance, their long ears erect. Two river-deer, with a strong smell of musk, sprang out from behind a big rock, with shy and affectionate eyes like those of a young girl in love. They walked towards the stream, breathing in deeply the mysterious air of Gokam. When they lifted their heads and looked up, they seemed as proud as princesses. From then on, everyday at sunset and sunrise Gokam became a watering-place for these animals.

When Cering Gyamo was two years old, she showed talents that ordinary children lacked. She had a relish for drawing sand tables on the ground. Mima had no idea that the pictures his daughter drew were actually totems showing the cycle of life and death in the human world. When she had just learned how to walk, she could dance a dance that had no regular pattern to follow. The foot marks she made on the sand could be interpreted as a constellation of stars which, unbeknown to Mima, were the footwork of a long-lost dance of a guardian warrior of the Yellow Sect of Lamaism. She could dance from "warrior-grade one" to "warrior-grade five". But all her supernatural talents were overpowered by the approach of strangers and, from that time she became one of the ordinary baby girls in the mountain region.

One day, when Caxun went to the brook to fetch water, she saw the head of a strange-looking man thrusting out from under a rock, with a moustache under his nose and a glowing white and pink complexion. Dropping her bucket with a scream, she rushed back her home, bolted the door and, in a hysterical voice, told Mima that she had seen a ghost. Mima asked if it was another wild man-like creature. Caxun said with a ghastly expression on her face that it was even more frightening and had red hair on his head. Holding Cering Gyamo tightly in their arms, the old couple knelt in front of the bronze statues placed on the earthen altar, and in trembling voices prayed for Bodhisattva to drive the ghost away and protect innocent lives. Cering Gyamo, however, cried desperately, trying to struggle free from their clasp.

Outside the cottage, a man, using language of respect, begged the host and hostess to open the door and receive the exhausted travellers. These respectful terms had been used by the aristocrats in Xalung County when he had taken two red fox-furs to the county magistrate there. When Mima opened the door, he did indeed see a red-haired ghost sitting on a rock, dressed in fantastic clothes with a big heavy bag on his back. His shoulders drooped and his hands rested on his knees. He looked exhausted. Next to him stood several bare-footed Tibetans, each with a heavy bundle on his back. After a while, another red-haired ghost, similar to the one sitting on the rock, crept up. He seemed to be very tired and, having exchanged a few words with the first one, fell on the grassy ground after climbing over a rock. He shook his head in agony and the first one bent over to pat his cheeks. Upon seeing Mima through the open door, they called out in perfect Tibetan and walked towards him. Within an hour or so, Mima's fear had evaporated and his vigilance had slackened. They told him they were not ghosts but two Englishmen investigating the course of the Yalu Tsangpo River and, following the river, they had arrived in the Pagbug region. They had walked along the foot of the mountain but they could not see any villages ahead. When they had looked through their binoculars, they had seen the village of Gokam nestling half-way on the hillside. They had decided to climb up and spend the night there because one of them was sick. The few Tibetan followers were serving their term of unpaid labour with them. The two Englishmen produced photos of the Thirteenth Dalai Lama and the Ninth Panchen Lama and showed them to Mima. Holding the photos in his hand, Mima was sceptical that these two mysterious Englishmen could carry with them the shadows of the Holy Monks. But when one of the Englishmen handed him a pair of binoculars and told him to look through them over the range of the mountain and the wide river in the south, Mima was amazed to see the scenes jumping right under his nose, the cow leather boat on the river and all. With his lips parted, he handed back the heavy black binoculars with trembling hands, convinced that the Englishmen had their own magic. While Caxun was busy making tea and cooking food for them, Mima noted that the colour of their eyes was strange — one of them had blue eyes and the other had grey ones. Over food, the Englishmen asked about the geography of the area. To please them, Mima, with renewed spirits, began to pour out story of the days when he was a young huntsman. They did not seem to be interested in his story, so they asked no more questions. After the meal, they paid for the food in Tibetan cash. Mima shook his head. He did not want their money. He wanted to have a jacket from them. After hesitating for a few moments, the Englishmen produced a semi-new, khaki army jacket from their knapsack and gave it to him.

Probably instinctively sensing something with the pheasants, the rabbits and the river deer stopped coming to Gokam to drink water. They stayed about a hundred yards away from the village, crying and calling in the rocks. The Englishman watched with interest and, taking out his revolver, aimed at the animals for a long while without pulling the trigger. The sick Englishman was carried to Wangme's dilapidated cottage and the Tibetan attendants dipped a piece of cloth in the stream and spread it over his forehead. Seeing that he might not survive that night, the kind-hearted Caxun knelt in front of the statue of Buddha and prayed for a long time. While the other Englishman sat by the fire, writing something in a notebook, all at once he was hit on the head by a pebble. Looking up, he saw the clever face of a young boy popping out from behind a rock. The Englishman asked Mima if the boy was his. When Mima shook his head, the Englishman became furious. Raising his pistol, he fired two shots into the sky. Mima was startled, but the Englishman said with a smile that he had fired merely to scare off the naughty child. By the next day the semi-conscious Englishman had recovered from his affliction as if he had never been seriously ill. Just as they were about to leave they noticed Cering Gyamo scuttling around between the legs of the adults. The Englishman who had recovered picked her up and, looking at her small dirty face with a certain measure of embarrass-ment, kissed her on the right cheek. The rough hairy kiss was like needles pricking her. Cering Gyamo burst into tears and rolled on the grass, her hands over her face. The group of explorers, headed by the Englishmen, left Gokam, climbing down the gentle rocky incline into the deep valley. Mima noticed that from time to time, they stumbled and fell to the ground, sometimes rolling over quite a distance with their knapsacks before they got up again. Seeing them fall and rise like that, Mima realized that people leaving Gokam with no intention of coming back all stumbled and fell as they went downhill. Wangme and his family had had falls going down; they would never come back and see their old neighbours again.

Of the two Englishmen, one was Colonel F.M. Bailey, member of the British Royal Geographical Society. He had come to Tibet with the British Expeditionary Forces and had been assigned to the Brit-ish Trade Delegate at Chunpi and Gyangze. Forty years later, he wrote *China — Tibet — Asam* and *A Trip to Tibet Without Passport*. The other was his assist-ant, Captain H.T. Morshead. During the First World

War a few years later, he became famous in Europe for surveying the Spitsbergen Islands. Later, he was murdered in Burma.

On Cering Gyamo's right cheek grew a reddish swelling from the kiss by Captain H. T. Morshead. The small holes pricked by the needle-like moustache were running with pus. The infuriated Mima let forth a volley of courses. Caxun, with great difficulty, climbed among the rocks gathering grass. She ground the blades to a pulp, mixed it with saliva and applied it to Cering Gyamo's face. Day and night she prayed for her to recover. Three days later, the reddish lump disappeared but, from then on, her eyes lost their usual mystical brilliance and she was no longer able to draw sand tables, let alone dance the mysterious guardian warrior's dances. In a word, all the mysterious signs she showed of being the incarnation of a saviour had gone, and only a few darkish moles remained on her face.

As soon as Cering Gyamo reached puberty, she began to show a propensity to wash herself in the stream. Every two or three days, she stripped down to her waist and knelt by the stream of the clear snow-water to wash her hair and her breasts. If she was not allowed to wash, she tore at her hair and clothes, groaning that she was feeling unbearably itchy. Her mother had tried all kinds of herbs on her but they had had no effect. Only a shower of cold water could ease the itching. Without knowing when, she began to become aware of her breasts growing hard and round on her chest. From then on, she couldn't help lifting her hands to caress them — the parts of the body that invariably produced mixed feelings of sadness and happiness. Suddenly, a pair of rough, powerful hands were thrust under her arms from behind, fingers clamping her nipples like pliers. Looking back over her shoulder, she saw a handsome young man — Dalang. Feeling an inner tingling sensation she closed her eyes without resisting. Dalang often took her unawares while she washed, getting hold of her from behind. He was perhaps twenty-seven or twenty-eight, with dishevelled hair and a dirty face. Having lived alone in the depths of the mountains, he had become very quick in his movements. But no one knew where he lived. He often came to flirt with Cering Gyamo, and Caxun, by now as old as a withered twig, would watch her daughter wrathfully through the door, howling with grief. Dalang would retreat from the scene when he heard her angry curses. And, of course, when she came home, the daughter was doomed to a severe reprimand from the mother. As Cering Gyamo grew into a beautiful young woman, the clothes she wore became shabbier by contrast and the flesh exposed through the worn-out parts forced her father to hang his head as if looking for ants on the floor. Unable to stand it any longer, he took out the green army jacket left behind by the Englishman a dozen years ago and threw it to his daughter. She put it on with admiration and, like magic, she no longer felt itchy, and so there was no need to wash again in the stream. She never took it off, not even once, until the day she died.

Once a month, her aged parents offered food to the great master practising lamaism in the secluded cave concealed by the interlaced undergrowth. Cering Gyamo had learned by watching how much fresh tea to put in the pot and how much fresh barley flour to put in the bag and how, without making the slightest noise, to bring out the empty pot and the leather bag and push in the newly-filled ones.

"How long has he been in there?" she asked.

"Only Budhisattva knows," her mother answered. "When we moved to Gokam forty years ago, an old man had just died. It was said he had been offering food to the great master all his life."

"Why doesn't he come out?"

"Peh!" Her mother spat in her face.

"You mustn't doubt the existence of this monk," her father explained. "His spirit can leave his body at any time, come out from the cave and fly around in the world. When you see a bird, or a horse, or a slight whirlwind blowing across in front of you, it could be the incarnation of the great master. So you mustn't do any harm to any living thing."

At the age of five, this was the first comprehensible conversation Cering Gyamo had had with her father. Since then she had known how to keep secret about the cave because her parents had been keeping on at her never to tell anybody else. Besides, Cering Gyamo was convinced that the great master was indeed inside the cave, for, upon returning from the cave, her mother would tell her husband excitedly that the great master had asked her questions. Sometimes he asked whether the water in the stream had turned muddy, and other times he asked whether any eagles had flown over head and other such insignificant questions.

Sometimes, Cering Gyamo looked lost in thought as she held a sleepy pheasant or a tame rabbit in her arms. She knew very well that, once her parents died,

Dalang would spring out from behind the rocks and force her to marry him. For ten years or so, he had been haunting the place like a ghost, stubbornly waiting for this day to arrive. However, Mima knew what to do to protect his daughter. After talking it over with his wife, one pitch-black night they took Cering Gyamo to the cave and knelt on the grassy ground in front of the black hole, praying to the mysterious great master to initiate their daughter into nunhood. They had agreed with Cering Gyamo that if there was no response from the cave, she could go her own way after they died. There was dead silence, the kind of silence that foreshadowed a miracle. Mima and his wife were just about to hang their heads in despair, when a strip of something, dimly whitish, floated out from the cave, a pure-white precious *hada* draped itself around Cering Gyamo's neck. Seeing what was happening, Mima clutched the front of his gown and said in a trembling voice, "This is a miracle! Isn't this a sign of initiation by the great master?" Cering Gyamo fainted to the ground, as if electrified. Her mother sprayed cold water over her forehead and, when she came to, they took her back to the cottage. That evening, by the dim light of the oil lamp they cut her long black shiny hair with an old but sharp hunting knife. Late that night, Mima breathed his last. Before he died, he uttered a heart-rending cry: "Triratna, the Buddha, the dharma and the sangha! After I'm gone, my beloved daughter Cering Gyamo will continue to serve you virtuously. Is this now my reward because in this life I did not do enough good nor accumulate enough wisdom?" And with these words he expired. According to astrological reckoning, Caxun should have lived another seven years but, on hearing her husband's agonized outcry, she departed with him. Caxun lived to be eighty-eight years old. After converting to Triratna, she steered clear of the feminine vices and exerted herself to do virtuous deeds. And so, the great sangha living in seclusion in the cave, while expiating her sins, arranged for a miracle to happen: Caxun's forehead split open and her brain sprang out, thus freeing her spirit to fly up to Heaven. And then her body rose as if raised by an invisible force until it landed on the spectacular peak of Mount Zela where a large flock of eagles stood waiting. Mima died at the age of ninety-two. His body floated out of the door, sank to the foot of the mountain and then down further still into the Yalu Tsangpo River.

Dalang, however, stood high upon a rock like an eagle, silently waiting for what seemed like three hours for Cering Gyamo to come out of the cottage. He stood there like a statue, sweating all over in the scorching sun. Finally Cering Gyamo walked out slowly, holding a bronze statue of Buddha in her hands, her head hanging low. She stood at the door, afraid to look up at him. When Dalang saw her clean-shaven head still bleeding, the bronze Buddha in her hands and the bright white *hada* around her neck, he sent a blood-curdling howl of grief up to heaven, expelling all the hardships he had suffered over the past eighteen years and the despair resulting from having waited for Cering Gyamo for so long.

One day in 1877, the twelve-year-old hunter Mima went hunting on top of Mount Sangzhapu. Behind him was a steep cliff and in front was a hillside overgrown with grass and at the far end of the grass several red foxes appeared. Soon they would come to drink from the stream not far from him. Suddenly his stomach began to churn violently and he felt he couldn't control his motions. Mima, hunter that he was, knew that foxes had a very sharp sense of smell. The morning breeze was blowing from behind, so, to keep the smell of defecation from reaching them, he quietly moved to the edge of the cliff. Pulling up the back of his gown and holding fast to a branch of a tree growing from a crack in the rocks, his body overhanging the cliff, with an effort he released the shit. It fell without the slightest echo of sound. Mima was filled with a sense of emptiness and unease when he moved away from the cliff. The red foxes were springing rhythmically towards him on their soft paws, claws outspread, their bodies cutting through the air. They landed agilely on the ground on their springy hindlegs and then jumped forward, their soft fluffy fur drifting buoyantly in the wind, their long thick tails streaming behind. He was enthralled by their graceful movements. When they arrived at the stream the foxes did not start drinking straightaway and so this was the best moment to shoot. Before Mima took aim, they began playing, chasing each other, and rolling on the ground, yelping with joy. Mima was strangely upset by the thought of his excrement drifting downward without over reaching the ground and this affected the instinctive composure and alertness of a skilled hunter. His eyes were dazzled by the foxes springing up and down like flames of fire. He was at the end of his patience. Holding the barrel of his musket, he nervously pulled the trigger.

A sharp crack split the air, ripping its way through to the mountains in the distance. The foxes, by instinct, crouched down and then shot off like lightning, sweeping upwards the tips of the blades of grass as they went, their long tails trailing over the grass. In an instant they had become tiny red dots in the distance and finally they disappeared over the horizon beyond the grassland. And then from the mountains opposite, a rumbling echo drifted back, like an awe-inspiring sigh evinced by the mountain god.

It was all silence again.

Mima was downcast. He dragged his feet towards the stream, his musket heavy in his hands. The game, so near at hand, had slipped through his fingers. This was the first failure ever inflicted upon this seasoned hunter. Something was wrong, but he could not make out what.

Sitting by the stream, he looked with blank eyes at the blades of grass which had glistened with dew early in the morning but now had become dark under the bouncing feet of the foxes as they had played around. Touching the grass with his big hands, it seemed he could still feel the warmth they had left behind. When he sniffed, he could still smell the irritating smell of the animals lingering in the air. He suddenly saw a fox's head popping up over a cluster of rocks and automatically raised his gun, about to shoot. When the illusion had passed, he saw on the huge rock a relief sculpture of Bodhisattva which had become blurred over the years with the slow erosion of nature. He walked nearer and found the spot of Bodhisattva's heart was blackened by smoke. He touched it with his finger and smelled it with his nose. It was gunpowder. He instant-

ly collapsed on the ground, as if suffering from unbearable cramps in his stomach.

That morning, Mima had done two wrongs, one of
which was shooting the mountain god, and the other
was that the excrement he had released eventually landed on the head of a hunter who was meditating at the
foot of the mountain. As a punishment, the village he
lived in was destroyed by a rockslide. Fortunately he
was prepared for this. When he heard the terrible
rumbling noise rolling down from the mountain, he
thrust a little money and some food into his wife's
hands and, lifting up his sick and aged mother, they
ran for their lives. In the darkness they stumbled towards the riverbank at the edge of the village. At daybreak, his mother died, and her body stiffened. He
knew this was the retribution they deserved. While he
washed her body in silence, a piece of white cloth
drifted down from the sky and landed on his mother's
shrunken chest. Picking it up he saw it was a *gatha*.
He tucked it into his pocket without showing it to his
wife. Having washed his mother, he knelt on the
ground and looked up at the sky. After saying in silence the six-word mantra forty-nine times, he pushed
his mother's body into the river, praying to the corpse
until it was out of sight. He took his wife by the hand
and walked into a valley of Mount Zela, as instructed
by the *gatha*. Climbing along a water-fall, they came to
a quiet village — Gokam. An old man had just died
and Mima joined in the funeral procession.

Mima and his wife settled there.

1929—1950

Mount Zela is located in the south of the Pagbug

ranges. It is a cone-shaped mountain, 16,000 feet above sea level with rows upon rows of peaks of different heights. With canyons and ravines running criss-cross, the mountain was rugged and rough. The poor soil had been washed away by the torrential rains in the summer and the land was left bare with outcrops of rocks and rows of cracks in the ground. The crops, like the patchy hide of a diseased cow, were sparse and stunted. Mountains rolled up and down along the old Yalu Tsangpo River. The top of Mount Zela was a vast desolate plain, strewn with hard blocks of earth and broken rock. One side of the plain was flanked by a snow-clad peak called Garong. When the snow melted, the water would flow through the gullies, off the eroded edges of the plain and then, passing the quiet village of Gokam situated in the valley, down to the foot of the mountain before it wound its way slow-ly through sandbanks into the river. On the other side of the plain was the precipitous cliff below which Bangdui Manor nestled out of sight. About five hun-dred yards away, there was another plain, much smaller in size. In the space of twenty minutes you could walk from one side to the other. Viewed from across the river, Mount Zela looked like two terraces side by side, and on top of the larger one, right in the middle, was a perfectly round lake reflecting the azure of the sky like a mirror. Around the lake a belt of green grass grew luxuriantly, an ideal place to farm any number of cows or sheep.

But no human being had ever set foot there until Dalang arrived.

Cering Gyamo was now the only villager left in Gokam. Apart from offering food to the great sangha practising lamaism in the cave, she had a few goats, a rabbit and a flock of pheasants to attend to. The goats grazed among the rocks every day and, as the grass was as low as patches of moss, they stretched their heads downwards as if they were nuzzling the ground. Dalang herded away fourteen of her goats from the top of the mountain, leaving her other possessions untouched, and did not even try to caress her for the last time.

Cering Gyamo seldom went down the mountain except to trade the butter she had made from the goats' milk for tea, salt and grain. She would often sit on the threshold of the cottage counting the beads of her rosary. While watching the sunrise and sunset, she tried to dimly recall her childhood. Although she could not recollect her parents' kind faces, she could clearly remember their voices. Whenever she wanted to hear something they had said, their words would ring out in her ears. Reliving memories of the past like this, she would quietly doze off against the door frame. Sometimes she would wake up with a start and look around, thinking Dalang was about to jump out from nowhere. She was now totally free. Since her mother had gone, no one would watch her through the door and no one would howl at her resentfully, but Dalang would never come. The young Cering Gyamo, standing up with a sigh, went back to her cottage, continuing to live her life with no sense of time in eternal loneliness.

As long as the tea pot and the leather bag were empty when she brought them out from the cave, she would never leave the deserted village of Gokam.

There was a black tent in the grass on the plain by

the lake and, viewed from a distance, it looked like a sleeping wild ox. Having lived through the two years of loneliness, accompanied only by the flock of goats, Dalang could endure it no longer. Every day, he would go to the eroded edge of the ravine between the plain and the mountain through which snow-water flowed into the canyon, and spend long hours watching the village of Gokam hidden in the valley. In the morning, he could see thin smoke curling up from below and Cering Gyamo's tiny figure moving about. When she walked into the shadows, he lost sight of her. Dalang often thought to himself that he should have taken her with him and asked her to live with him, but he knew it was not possible. Inhaling a deep breath of the unpolluted mountain air, he made up his mind to go down the other side of the mountain.

Late autumn, he came back, with an attractive young woman. Dalang, a rifle slung over his shoulder, walked in front, twisting woollen threads and the woman, ready to follow him anywhere, was leading a horse loaded with all the household necessities they would need on top of the mountain. This woman had been the prestigious, respectable young wife of the general manager of a county magistrate. She had given birth to three girls all at once and, this had caused panic and fear among the people for several hundred miles around. They swarmed to the temple and, kowtowing, demanded that the lamas subdue the female demon from hell. An exorcizing ritual was held on the open ground in front of the temple. The lamas, having chanted incantations for one day and one night, brought her to the temple in the morning, perched facing backwards on the back of an old donkey her hands tied up behind her. People from a dozen villages around had come, on horseback or on foot, to see what was going to happen to her. Her three dead babies, wrapped in mud, were placed in three pots and buried in the ground and then a white rock was placed on top of them to keep the evil creatures in hell forever. The spectators craned their necks to see what the lamas were going to do with this pretty coquettish woman. Dalang happened to pass the temple and joined the crowd out of curiosity. The elderly lama gestured at two middle-aged women to remove her clothes and the women, furious as irritated apes, kept spitting into her face and dancing around her like furies, while they pulled off her clothes. She stood naked in the middle of the ground, stoic as if lost in recollection. The crowd gave a roar of laughter. Dalang was enamoured of the woman's naked body, his eyes bloodshot. He frantically broke into the crowds, and swinging around a long stick he had picked up somewhere, and uttering unfathomable shrieks, he sent the spectators, the executing lamas and allrunning for their lives, screaming that they had seen a monster. Dalang picked up the woman and knocking down an official transfixed to the spot with fear, put her on the white horse standing next to him and galloped off, taking with him the rifle he had grabbed from the official. All the way back he was beside himself with joy, the back of the naked woman rubbing against his bare chest. He was inspired by a manly pride in conquest — a feeling he had never had before. He had been wanting to have a woman that could produce offspring for him like a rabbit. They lived on the quiet remote plain of Mount Zela, intoxicated by love. The woman did not let him down. In just a short period of time, she bore him five children, two of whom died in infancy and the others, with pretty plump faces, grew under their parents' tender protection against the scorching sun and the fierce dry winds of the highland, into three healthy boys.

One unusually dark night, a spring wind arose up on the horizon and, bearing the fresh and fragrant air of the valley, came sweeping along with tremendous force, bringing life and vitality to everything it passed. It rolled freely across the highland, howling with delight. The wind swirled around, spreading darkness throughout the space between the valley and the sky. As it blew, it picked up fist-sized stones from the ground and hurled them like shooting stars, thus demonstrating to Mother Nature its irresistable force.

Dalang and the woman sat in the protection of the dark tent and their children, careless of the roaring wind that rocked the world, wandered around in their dreamland of childhood. The spring wind, like a prankish adult, violently shook the small tent as if determined to transport the whole stranded family to the other side of the horizon. The tent stood alone on the boundless plain, swaying back and forth in the frenzied wind; it had become one with the highland, firmly planted in the solid ground. Inside the narrow tent, the man and the woman sat in silence, listening to the vigorous sounds of nature. Though they could not see each other, they testified to each other's existence by calling to each other with their hearts. The spring wind awakened their emotions and desires that had been suppressed by snow and ice throughout the winter. Blood surged through their veins like water rushing down the rivers.

"My dear wife, please feel my heart with your hand." He took her soft hand in his and put it to his bare chest.

"Oh, Dalang, Dalang," the woman called out in excitement, edging closer to him in the dark.

The night was as black as ink. The deathly silence following the last gust of wind across the highlands was as stifling as that of a dreamlike world. They felt as if they were dizzily rising into the night sky. They strained desperately to hear the slightest sound. It was a moment of painful expectation. Finally they heard a faint sound, a real sound, floating up from some remote place. It was like an animal shrieking at one moment and a baby crying at another. Dalang and his woman, hand in hand, came out from the tent, and stood in the moon light reflecting from an opening in the clouds. They remained there with no clothes on, bathing their strong bodies in the crystal flood of light. They stood listening, transported by the sound that came from nowhere.

"You see, we are not lonely," Dalang said, warmly holding the woman's cool and slippery shoulders in his arms. "Mount Zela is like the Divinity in Heaven. It has bestowed much on us. There are lives around us and the spirit presents itself everywhere. It is always with us, above our heads, under our feet. Why do we need to see it with our eyes? I hear it, I smell it and I feel it here." He pointed his finger at his heart.

Cering Gyamo picked a blade of grass and held it up in the first joint of her thumb. When she straightened her thumb again, the blade was firmly caught there. She turned until her thumb pointed towards a wide space in the south so that she could tell what time it was by looking where the shadow of blade pointed. This she had learned from her father. She looked for a while but there was no shadow cast on the back of the thumb. She was puzzled. She had no idea it was half past six, on the thirtieth day of the tenth month of the year of the water-chicken according to the Tibetan calendar. She spread a handful of barley-grain to the pheasants and went inside to sit on a goatskin. She took the rosary from her wrist and started counting the beads. When she heard someone calling her in a low voice from outside, she was scared, because, for years, Gokam had not been visited by a single person. With her heart in her mouth, she got up slowly to open the door. It was Dalang. The same Dalang with curly hair on his head and a long nose above his upper lip, his eyes sparkling. He was as handsome as ever.

"Are you here to mortify me again? You must know that I have become a nun," she said with difficulty.

"No, I am not. You have been molested by many men." He was disgusted, his thick lips twisted into a knot.

"Except for you, no one else has ever touched me and Bodhisattva knows that," Cering Gyamo called out, feeling wronged.

"I am so hungry, you haven't offered me food for the last three days." He produced from inside his loose robe the empty tea pot and the dry and shrunken leather bag and put them at her feet.

"Oh! My Triratna! Are you the one my family has

been offering food to generation after generation?'' she asked in surprise.

"You knew from the beginning that I wouldn't go too far from you. I often go without food. Perhaps I'll be better off next spring.'' Embarrassed, he held his head low.

"Oh, Dalang!'' Cering Gyamo seemed to have so much to reproach him with. "Why are you always haunting me like a ghost?''

"Even when I was very small, you held me in your arms and asked me to be your woman when I grew up. If I had been able to speak then, I would have said I was afraid. When I was older, you often took your chance with me by the river and made me become infatuated with you. When you left Gokam, you herded away a large flock of my goats. I thought, after that, I would be free from all feminine emotions and desires, but every night I am troubled by wicked and shameful dreams, for you have been hiding in my head like a ghost. You went to the top of the mountain not to stay away from me but to conquer me from above and weigh me down with Mount Zela until I suffocate to death. Do you deny you are not trying to manipulate me?'' she said with bitter tears in her eyes.

"All right. Since you put it that way, you ought to be brave enough to leave Gokam and come and live with me on the top of the mountain.''

"No! I cannot leave,'' she said in panic.

"Today I've come all the way to see you but, instead of giving me a tiny bit of food to eat, you've showered me with reproaches. Damn this wicked place.'' He took out his flint, with a rapid glance around. "I am going to set this place on fire and burn it down.''

Impassively, Cering Gyamo watched Dalang light the cotton with the flint and transfer the flame to a strip of cloth. Then he set light to a heap of dry grass, added some firewood, and the fire began to soar upwards. In an instant, Gokam was engulfed by the surging smoke and Cering Gyamo was lost in it. Dalang, however, disappeared from the scene. Cering Gyamo, as if awakening from a dream, her flesh licked by the tongues of fire, tried to escape from the smoke. Choked by the dense fumes, she had no strength to utter a sound. She felt she was sinking into the burning fires of hell and she called for help desperately: I am going, I am going. Please stop torturing me, Bodhisattva! Please get me out of the fire! Suddenly, beautiful sounds, like Buddhist music, drifted down from the sky and an indistinct voice said: If your soul is still lingering behind, what's the use of departing just with your body?

The night was extremely dark and the air was humid. The water in the stream gurgled along as if it had got something to tell and it seemed it wouldn't stop murmuring until its message was someday understood. It seemed as though every rock and every plant in the quiet canyon was straining its eyes to learn the secret of the night, but they would keep quiet about what they saw forever.

Cering Gyamo was exhausted. She managed, however, to crawl to the earthen altar on which stood the statue of Buddha. She stirred the ashes of the oil lamp and it became brighter. She picked up a bowlful of clear holy water and carefully looked at herself in it. She was still young, only twenty-three years old, with

a pair of large bright eyes and a pretty nose. Around
the corners of her mouth a pair of dimples faintly revealed a subtle expression. The few light brown tiny
specks on her right cheek were the marks branded on
her skin by the Englishman when she was two years
old. When she looked up at the dim wall, she saw
rows of strokes on it, some horizontal, some vertical
and others slanting. These were the record of the days
gone by, revealing something mysterious. When she
counted the fresh strokes she had made, she somehow
realized that, for three days, she had not been to the
cave to offer food to the great sangha.

At midnight, holding a corner of her skirt with her
hand, she picked her way to the cave. The black
clouds blocking the moon were like exotic rocks formed
into strange-looking peaks. The smaller clouds around
the moon were the shapes of the sharp claws and long
teeth of beasts and ghosts. They were like dire pictures
of hell hanging upside down from the sky. Suddenly,
her heart missed a beat and she almost dropped the
tea pot in her hands, for she heard a real clear voice
asking from the cave, "Have you seen any dharma-
protectors descending from Heaven?"

Cering Gyamo, spellbound, did not answer. Her legs
weakening, she fell on the ground prostrate.

"You are the incarnation of Yogacara Dakini."
The stony voice revealed her origin. Unprepared for
this, she remained speechless for a long while.

The rest of the message was unfathomable. At one
moment, the mysterious rhythm was like gurgling water, at another, it was like the groans of sea-tides. However, she was sure of one thing: at this minute she
stood at the cave not as Yogacara Dakini, but as an

ordinary mortal in the mundane world. Instinctively
she sensed that that night she was going to be the one
in whom both catastrophic agonies and a dreamlike
holy state of transcendence would be incarnated. It was
a most secret confidential revelation of which the fire
she had dreamed was but the omen.

"It's too bright outside," the voice became ani-
mated. "Is it fire or polar light?"

"Respected Master," Cering Gyamo began to tremble as if she had caught malaria. She was drifting into
a delirium.

"It's too bright there, too bright," the voice said
aloud. "Block out the light. Block it out. I am afraid.
Block it out, please."

Cering Gyamo crawled towards the mouth of the
cave and blocked it with her body, her arms out-
stretched.

The moon glided out of the clouds, casting the clear
cold light of a sword of steel.

Cering Gyamo was motionless, as if firmly transfixed
to the rock with an arrow shot from behind.

She was bathed in moonlight.

Dalang sat in the tent, cleaning the Russian-made
rifle. As it was seldom used, the barrel had become
rusty and it took him a long while to rub it until it
shone again. His woman was making cow-dung cakes
to dry on a stone outside the tent, with the oldest son
and the youngest one helping her. The second son,
Tashi Nyima, was engrossed in watching his father
cleaning the gun. Suddenly, a thunderous rumble was
heard from the sky and Dalang burst out of the tent.
Before he had time to look up and see where it came
from, his woman shrieked behind him in a ghastly

voice. A gigantic magic bird such as they had never seen before was flying in circles overhead, uttering an ear-splitting noise. It seemed to be trying to find somewhere to land. The children dashed back into the tent, like rats running from an owl. Tashi Nyima, however, called to the "bird" while his mother tried to drive the monster away by shouting, spitting and clapping her hands.

"You mustn't come down! Away with you, you devil!" Dalang was angry. He raised his gun and fired a few shots towards the monster. The bird-like giant glided round in circles overhead several times before it flew towards the east, uttering a long agonising groan.

This was a four-engined transport plane belonging to the US Air Force. During the Second World War, it flew to China via India while carrying out a mission against the Japanese army. Having flown off course and run out of fuel, the plane was going to land on this ideal natural landing place on top of Mount Zela. Threatened by the shots from down below, it flew away. Finally the plane crashed at a sandy place called Duo, not far from Samye Temple east of Mount Zela. The body of the plane slanted down and its right wing sank deep into the sand, but the American pilot, Croshiel, survived. After some investigation, the wreckage of the plane was abandoned there. Later, some local people put up a wooden post and tied a broken piece of the wing to the top. In the 1960s, somebody took it down and made it part of his collection.

It was the first time that the Tibetans had seen an aeroplane.

When Dalang appeared on the horizon of the plain,

the woman and children, with their eyes shaded from the sun with their hands, were all looking in his direction. He was carrying a game animal almost as long as himself, his gun barrel shining behind above his head.

"Oh! What a big river-deer," his oldest son, Tashi Dawa, commented.

"Doesn't look like a river-deer. It's more like a yak," the second son Tashi Nyima said.

"Did he steal it from somewhere?" the youngest son asked.

"Stop talking nonsense! Go and help him," their mother ordered.

The oldest and the youngest dashed off to meet their father and Tashi Nyima stood behind, watching them calmly.

What he was carrying on his shoulder was a dying man covered with blood. His blood oozed onto Dalang's back, staining it red. "Had I known he was dying, I wouldn't have carried him all the way up here. I am not a master of celestial funerals." He dumped the dead body by the tent and seated himself on the grass, gasping for breath. He was already in his fifties, and was beginning to feel his age.

At the foot of the mountain, while he was hiding behind the rocks, he had watched a fierce battle between a band of robbers and caravan of traders. The bandits, taking shelter among the rocks, fired volleys of bullets at the merchants as they passed through the valley. They were all good shots. The first volley felled three merchants at a range of several hundred feet and the rest of them hurriedly blew whistles and the well-trained mules, loaded with boxes of woollen clothes, wrist watches, gold coins and other precious articles, all crouched down on the ground in a semi-circle. They fired back at the bandits, taking shelter behind their mules, but the bandits avoided the animals and aimed at the men. After a few minutes' stalemate the bandits jumped onto their horses and, shouting and swinging the knives in their hands, charged downhill. Unable to block their savage attack, the merchants abandoned their mules and ran for their lives, but they were cut off by the charging robbers and became locked in a dagger fight. When one young man, having killed several bandits, was about to go to rescue his father who had been knocked down by the horses, he was stabbed several times from behind and, finally, fell over his father's corpse groaning with pain. The robbers tied the corpses of their men to the horses and galloped away, taking with them the caravan's mules. When quietness at last prevailed, Dalang came out from behind the rocks and the scene he witnessed was more revolting than that of a gun-battle. Seeing that the legs of the young man were still twitching, he picked him up and carried him back over his shoulder.

The man was fortunate enough to survive his fatal wounds, and he regained consciousness that night. The three boys expected to find a fortune on him and they did find, in addition to a German-made Mauser and a few gold women's necklaces, a large pile of Indian rupees with the image of King Edward on them. To Dalang and his family who lived on top of Mount Zela, apart from the pistol which appealed strongly to the youngest son, the rest were not worth much. While the youngest son was fiddling with the pistol, he accidentally discharged it. The bullet went off from under

Tashi Dawa's arm, flew past in front of Dalang who was drinking tea in the tent and, ripping the canvas, hit the head of a goat that was grazing by the lake. The goat fell heavily on the grass, blood oozing into the lake.

Three months later, the young man recovered. He had twenty-seven knife-scars all over his body and a bullet scratch on the inside of his thigh. On his head alone there were three scars, one crossing diagonally from the right-hand corner of his forehead down to the left-hand corner of his jaw. The whole face was a distorted image as if reflected from a broken mirror. He was from Kamba, a member of the wealthy merchant, the famous Jamlojin's caravan. When he parted, he took only the pistol with him, leaving all the other possessions to Dalang and his family. From then on, he said, he would take to the forests, looking for the enemy who had killed his father. To thank Dalang for saving his life and the woman for her careful nursing, he promised, in twenty days, to bring back a bagful of gold coins with which they could buy a luxurious house in Lhasa and, if they wished, a position of an official, so that they could enjoy all human luxuries for the rest of their lives.

"Don't bother about that. Gold coins are not necessarily as important to us up here as the hay we need for the winter," Dalang said.

"My dear saviour, tell me what you want." His deformed face looked hideous.

"As you see, my sons are grown. They are full of energy, like young bulls. They often fight like mad and hurt each other for with no reason at all." Dalang squinted at the grassy ground where the three robust, stocky, dark-complexioned boys were challenging each other to a test of strength around a large smooth boulder.

Three days later, the man returned, leading a horse carrying a woman, two bagfuls of salt, cloth and other daily articles on its back. The three boys, attending the goats by the lake, watched the man coming up. They knew why the woman had been brought to them, but none of them moved. The young man from Kamba handed over the reins of the horse to Dalang and said, "May Bodhisattva bless you with a good fortune and a happy life." He left the woman and the horse with Dalang and, without taking any tea, headed straight off towards the edge of the plain.

"Cering Gyamo! Was this predestined in our previous lives?" Dalang looked at young woman in front of him, his eyes filled with tears. "You cut your long pretty hair many years ago, why have you come back to me now with your charming features of an angel to remind me of the things of the old days?"

Stroking the mane of the horse with her hand, the girl looked at the boys, not knowing which one she would belong to that night. She said with embarrassment, "Thank you for discovering my name by magic, but I've never cut my hair from my head and I've never seen you either during the day or in dreams at night."

When Dalang had calmed down, he looked embarrassed in front of his daughter-in-law to be. "Well, well. Don't take it seriously. As a matter of fact, I was...."

Dalang's woman, like a gust of wind, swirled up to the girl from nowhere. "Ah! Do you know how to milk cows?''

"Yes.''

"Do you know how to make butter, cut cloth and cook?''

She nodded her head.

"Can you chant Buddhist scriptures?''

"I ... I'm illiterate.''

"That's all right.'' The woman held her shoulders warmly. "That's not very important so long as you can conceive children.''

Cering Gyamo spent that night in the boys' tent, thus becoming their wife.

Dalang had become much older. His skin had turned loose and his eyes were devoid of lustre. During the day, he would fall into a trance, often whispering to the dogs, the ropes of the tents and even the cowdung. At breakfast, with shaky hands, he would upset the tea Cering Gyamo brought him. When walking in the meadows, he would stumble and fall but, when he got up and looked behind him, there was nothing there. When Cering Gyamo walked past him, with a pail in her hand and her sleeves rolled up, he always smelled the wet and mildewy smell typical of Gokam.

"Damn it!'' he cursed losing his temper.

One day, Cering Gyamo decided to do some physical work, to put an end to her peaceful daily routine. She began to take down the rocks from the broken walls of the four or five deserted cottages and neatly piled them on the grassy ground. She dismantled the rotten beams and door frames and put them beside the rocks. She had worked for a whole year and cleared all the dilapidated houses except the one she lived in.

She knew that very soon, Gokam would be visited by strangers, whether she liked it or not, and she would hate to present a desolate picture of the place.

When it occurred to her that she had not taken a bath for many years, she took off her clothes and with some hesitation went into the icy water. She did not feel like shouting with excitement as she did in the good old days. Without that passionate enthusiasm, she ran her hands over her slackening skin and shrunken breasts. Under the transparent water, the shape of her body looked like something grotesque. Suddenly, she saw a violent blast of wind blow up at the foot of the mountain, sweeping up clouds of dust in which a row of men in dark clothes appeared to be moving across the sand dunes. Changing its direction, the wind crept up along the rocks, and with a dreadful roar, rumbled across the valley. Standing motionless in the water, Cering Gyamo was held in thrall by the extraordinary phenomenon. When she saw a piece of red cloth fluttering in the air and moving in the direction of Gokam, she became very excited. She was convinced that it was a gatha from heaven. As the red cloth glided overhead, she jumped out of water and grabbed it with her hands. It was rectangular, about half the size of her room, with some bright yellow signs embroidered on it, the meaning of which she could not make out. Before she knew what was happening, the red cloth slipped out of her hands. Flying up and down a few times, it swept off downhill along with a gust of swirling wind.

It was a red flag with several Chinese characters which read: "March Towards Tibet!"

The white stone, as large as a cow's head, had been moving imperceptibly. It moved more slowly than the shadow of the moon. If you fixed your eye on it for a long moment, you had the feeling that it was just like any other stone that had been lying there for many years. If you turned your eyes away from it or came back after finishing a minor chore, you would find that it had moved forward a bit. Dalang discovered this by accident. One night, when he got up and went out to piss, he stumbled over the stone outside the tent. He had never seen it there before. At first he thought Cering Gyamo had put it there to crush the leg-bones of cows to extract marrow for making soup, but the next morning he found it had moved towards the boys tent. He kept quiet about it.

Being a virtuous wife, Cering Gyamo did her best to satisfy the demands of her three husbands. By taking good care of them, she got them as tame as sheep so that they lived together in perfect harmony and delight. At dawn, she was the first to get up and went about making tea. She filled the earthenware pot with tea and took it to her parents-in-law. She then brought what was left back to her husbands. She set the *tsamba* and other foods out on the low table, then went to the pen with a pail in her hand to milk the cows. She scattered the first ladleful of milk into the air with a prayer. When Dalang's woman got up, she also scattered some butter tea in the direction of the boundless plain, and called, at the top of her voice, the names of Sakyamuni and other gods for their blessings. Her voice was so loud that it carried right across to the end of the plain. After breakfast, the sons untied the reins and, whistling, cracking whips and throwing pebbles, ran the cows and goats to the lake and let them wander about to graze freely in the flourishing grass. The lambs and calves were tied around the tents. Cering Gyamo made cakes with the cow-dung from the night before and dried them in the sun to be used as fuel.

Cering Gyamo found herself more attached to Tashi Nyima, the second of the three. He was not very strong compared to the other two, nor was he especially talented, but he had a pair of deep and melancholy eyes with which he would, as he stood alone by the pastureland, gaze fixedly at the mountains in the distance. From the way he looked, she discerned that his disturbed heart was flying across the plain, over Mount Zela and to the unknown world beyond. At night, she enjoyed putting her ear to his bare chest which gave her a sense of security the way an impregnable city wall did for its citizens. She sank into her dreamland with his vigorous and rhythmical heartbeat which sounded like the footsteps of eternal life. Though his heartbeat was not like the beating of a drum, it produced intriguing notes imbued with constant longings and yearnings and sorrowful emotions. Cering Gyamo was overcome by a sense of anticipation that Tashi Nyima would become someone admirable and great. His spirit distilled itself in the world of illusion he had created for himself. He would not be left in obscurity like a lonely wind that swirled around on the plain and finally disappeared off its edge. Some day, he would be like an eagle flying far and wide, up in the sky.

When the white stone was about five or six feet from the tent, Dalang thought the time had come. He told

Tashi Nyima to go down the mountain, taking a large flock of goats, several yaks, bagfuls of butter and cheese and several dozen pieces of soft leather to trade for salt, tea, grain, cloth and daily necessities from the peasants there. The other two boys also wanted to go and see the outside world, but Dalang wouldn't let them. As winter was approaching, there was a lot of work to do. They had to transfer the four hundred goats, eighty yaks and the several dozen horses to the grassland below the snow-clad mountain and herd them back to the lake when there was not much grass left. There were more chores for them. The men, while attending the livestock, had to twist woollen threads and rub the oil-soaked leather. Dalang's woman and her oldest son stayed at home, taking care of the lambs and calves and weaving wool carpets. The able-bodied men had to slaughter goats and yaks and, after drying the meat, store it for the long winter. Autumn was a busy season.

With the consent of his parents and brothers, Cering Gyamo went down the mountain together with Tashi Nyima because as a housewife she knew better what they needed at home.

Five days later, Dalang found, when he walked out of the tent, the white stone had moved inside the boys' tent. As usual, Cering Gyamo went to milk the cows with a pail in her hand. She had returned at midnight with all the things they had planned to trade, so Tashi Dawa told his father. But Tashi Nyima had not come back with her and she said in panic that she had never gone down the mountain with anybody by the name of Tashi Nyima. Since she had come to Mount Zela, everything she had known about the outside world had slipped from memory. The only thing she was aware of was that she had been living happily with two husbands and there was never anyone else in her life. Patting her bulging belly, she asked her husbands: have I passed any night without sleeping in this tent? They quickly pushed such a perplexing question to the back of their minds because they didn't want to rack their brains about the whys and wherefores. Besides they didn't have the time. Since yesterday was already gone, what had happened in the past was but a dream. Right now they were up to their necks in work. All this could wait to be reasoned out when they didn't have to struggle for a living, in other words, when they were old and sitting at the door of the tent, with a prayer wheel of Buddhist scriptures in their hands. Then they would recall the countless events that had happened to them and the hardships they had suffered, while praying to heaven with eyes closed.

Dalang felt a great sense of relief, as if dark clouds had lifted and he spat a little saliva to the ground contentedly. That night he said a long long prayer, kneeling in front of the bronze statue of Buddha by the light of the lamp that burned day and night. But the next day he had a sore under his nose and it tormented him for five days running.

1953—1985

Dalang gestured to his two sons to drop their guns and he lowered the barrel of his, because they were outnumbered by far and their weapons were inferior. Only the two fierce yellow dogs with red collars kept barking frenziedly at the strangers, baring their sharp teeth. When the dogs were chained up, they grew desperate and started digging two pits in the ground with their claws.

A peasant from the valley interpreted for the man in khaki uniform with a pistol slung over his shoulder. He tried to alleviate the nervousness and hostility of Dalang and his family by saying that they were the People's Liberation Army and they had come to relieve the people of their sufferings and hardships. The guide talked a lot. Finally he produced a letter and handed it over to Dalang. In the letter there was a photo, a photo of Tashi Nyima who was in exactly the same khaki uniform as the soldier's. With the presentation of the photo, their hostility instantly melted away and Dalang invited them inside the tent. They were warmly received by the herdsmen. Tashi Dawa and his brother Norbu Tseten both wanted to look at the photo first and they were amazed when they saw their brother's face printed on the glossy paper.

They called Cering Gyamo to them and asked, "You said you have never known any other man in your life, don't you remember Tashi Nyima? Didn't you go down the mountain with him?"

"I swear to Triratna I don't know this man in the photo. No, I really don't." She was so baffled that there were tears in her eyes.

"Well, don't worry. It's not important that you don't know him. We have a brother anyway. We three were brought up together by our mother. This picture reminds us of the eventful past. Cering Gyamo doesn't know this man, it's all right. But how come you don't know him? Well, don't worry. Go and make tea for the guests."

Tashi Nyima said in his letter that not long after descending the mountain, he had joined the revolutionary army and had won honours for outstanding services. He and his wife Cering Gyamo were going to study at a school to learn more about the world — there was wonderful life ahead of them. At the end of the letter he said he missed his parents and brothers every day.

The Liberation Army had come to grant agricultural loans. They gave Dalang and his family some silver dollars and an embroidered silk portrait. They told Dalang the man in the portrait was Mao Zedong.

For the whole afternoon Dalang was absorbed in the portrait, studying it from different angles. When Tashi Dawa rushed in, telling him that the two cows were about to give birth, Dalang followed him out, in excitement. Two calves were born without any difficulty and Dalang took it as a good omen. Back in the tent, he took another look at the portrait with the conviction that it had brought him good luck and, with great respect he hung it over the altar. He called the army Bodhisattva-sent soldiers and, strange enough, many Tibetans called the soldiers in the same way, so they said.

Tashi Dawa the oldest son was eager to go down the mountain with the soldiers. When they asked Dalang if he would let him go, he was tongue-tied. "Are there any women down the mountain?" Tashi Dawa asked. "Yes!" The soldiers were embarrassed. "There are many beautiful healthy peasant girls there." Tashi Dawa asked his brother and Cering Gyamo to stay and take care of their aging parents while he was away with the army. He told his father he wouldn't go any further than Bangdui and he would come back and visit them often. Dalang acquiesced. Life was different now. Mount Zela was no longer as deserted as it had been decades ago. Outside the tent on the grass, his grandchildren were playing with the sheep dogs that were bigger than the children themselves.

Visitors had recently come to Gokam but they had only found one lonely old woman in exotic attire. When they saw a pile of rocks and a pile of wood neatly arranged, they were puzzled. They had tried to talk her into moving down the mountain saying that the people down there did not have to do any unpaid labour or pay any taxes and, if she went there, she would be assisted by the local government in one way or another. Cering Gyamo accepted the things they brought to her but refused to leave her home.

Tashi Dawa was elected chairman of the poor peasants' association and he visited Gokam more often than others. Every time he was there, he gazed on a stream flowing through Gokam down the mountain. Parted by the round boulders in the upper reaches, the water trickled carefully through the rocks before it converged into one stream again. Dodging the stones to the right and left, the water sometimes overflowed the boggy mossy banks and sometimes ran off the cliffs down into the valley. As it crashed onto the hard rocks, it sent snow-like foam flying up, the clear rapid stream turning into a muffled rumbling in the deep valley. When the water flowed over the grassy plain of Gokam, the ripples pushed each other over the grass and, reaching the edge of the plain, ran right off the cliff down into a deep pool.

Tashi Dawa's mind was wandering.

"Now I know. You can see Gokam from the top of

the mountain," he murmured to himself. "No wonder every day he went to sit there for a while."

"Who went to sit at the top?" Cering Gyamo asked.

"My father, Dalang."

"Are you Dalang's son?"

"Yes."

"I see."

"Are you?"

"He is old and so am I." Cering Gyamo closed her eyes. "But no one knows for how long the water has been flowing like this, and the old days are all gone with it."

"Ahma, you don't know what I am thinking about. The water...."

"Don't say it, my child. Don't say it. The water is proof that there were people living in Gokam before. You don't know much about that." She stopped with a sigh. She knew she would live here until the day when she would quietly leave the world because for so many years, she had found the tea pot and the food bag empty when she brought them out from the cave. She was destined, in this life, to look after the great sangha in the cave by offering him tea and food. That night over thirty years ago when the moon was obscured by black clouds shaped like strange mountains, the master in the cave, having completed the mysterious rituals, had issued such instructions: "From now on, try to live through the world of loneliness and the seas of miseries and you'll achieve goodness. Do your best, continue to be virtuous and believe in the Triratna, and eventually you will be fortunate and contented." A metallic clanking sound had issued from the cave, and then silence.

One day, a large team of peasant labourers came down to Gokam from the mountain. Tashi Dawa, the secretary of the commune Party branch, walked in front, holding a red banner in his hands. It had been his ambition for years to involve the commune members in the construction of a reservoir, thus turning snow-water to the advantage of the liberated serfs — a symbol that nature could be transformed by man. Instantly, the birds and animals around Gokam all swarmed away. For over one hundred days and nights there was the banging of hammers, the noise of explosives going off in chorus, and the sound of drills and spades. The site, dotted with flags, slogans and torches, was full of rumbling crowds of people singing vibrant songs. Gokam had awoken from thousands of years of sleep. Cering Gyamo, now bedridden, was haunted by nightmares day and night. The project progressed towards the edge of the high rock. Whenever she heard the noise of the drills on the rock she would feel reassured. But the workers, in one way or another, kept away from the rock, for the reservoir was to be located some distance in front of it. The rocks Cering Gyamo had put aside were all used to line the bottom. The scene was one of enthusiasm and excitement, some turning rocks, some digging pits, some building the dam and some ramming the earth. A newly-dug irrigation ditch wound around the mountain like a giant snake. As the dam rose up day by day, the water rose with it, forming a small lake. The water ran over the foundations of the houses long abandoned by their owners. Cering Gyamo's house, however, was at a higher point, about ten feet from the lake and the cave, of course, was not disturbed either.

Something mysterious was happening. During the day, the reservoir filled up with water and was kept in by the gate but at night the water leaked out, so that only a little muddy water remained at the bottom. Since it didn't flow into the irrigation ditch, nor leak out into the canyon through the base of the dam, how then did the water disappear? It was mysterious. Tashi Dawa looked, with suspicious eyes, at the ankle-deep water, not knowing what to do. Someone reported that some bad elements resentful of being put under surveillance had spread rumours that Mount Zela was a divine mountain and it was the will of divinity to channel the snow-water into the river, so it was hardly worth trying to change its course. The water leaked out through the bottom and flowed out into the river. Tashi Dawa held a meeting and commune members discussed ways and means of transforming the rough barren land into cultivatable fields.

One peasant at the discussion drank tea out of a plastic bag instead of a bowl. While he was drinking, the bag broke and the tea splashed all over the peasant next to him. It suddenly occurred to Tashi Dawa that the plastic bag broke because the tea was hot, but the water from the snow-clad mountain was always cold. The moment his bold idea was put forward at the Party branch meeting, it was accepted at once. They arranged for several tractors to go to the county town and bring back several dozen rolls of plastic sheeting. The team of peasant labourers carried the sheeting and went up to Gokam for a second time. The skilled workers joined the sheets into one large piece by burning the edges and pressing them together with heated iron rods. They covered the bottom of the reservoir with thirteen of the large sheets, sealing the joints firmly to the rocks with cement. This miracle, it was said, was unprecedented in history. It was accomplished solely by the highly enthusiastic peasant masses without the assistance of experts, designers, or technical personnel. They did not even have designs to work from, or the necessary machines or equipment. The leakage problem solved, the water, passing forty-nine bends along the mountain, flowed to the small plain, 4,800 metres above sea level, next to the Zela plateau. Three thousand *mu* of the plain was covered with spongy, rich soil which the peasants had carried in conical wicker crates from the rich fields at the foot of the mountain. Each peasant could undertake only three journeys up and down a day, each crate containing only two spadefuls of earth. Like ants carrying food, the peasants moved ninety percent of the land's top layer up to the mountain. The next autumn, a miracle — six hundred catties of wheat per *mu*, was produced on the highest fields in the world.

From then on, Bangdui Commune became famous — the name of Bangdui and its people hit the headlines — and cadres and reporters in the town swarmed to this place to see what was happening. Naturally, the reservoir was one of the things they wanted to see most of all. The visitors, wearing straw hats, equipped with food and water, spent two hours in the scorching sun, climbing up to the plain to see the three thousand *mu* of wheat and then spent another two hours walking along the irrigation ditch to visit the reservoir. The young guide from the commune stood at the dam and recited her explanation, like a school girl mechanically saying a text from memory. Each time she explained, she spent twenty-seven minutes, no more, no less. The visitors would produce their notebooks and jot down almost every word she said about the great accomplishment, while muttering sounds of surprise and admiration. Then there was a short break during which everyone would go to the lowest stone step to scoop up some water with their hands which was said to be as sweet as dew. Some marked their names on the rocks with nail-clippers or scissors and others had photos taken. Before leaving, some would fill their water-bottles with the water to take back as precious presents for their friends or relatives.

Somebody caught sight of an old woman with a lifeless expression on her face like a ghost, sitting in front of a ramshackle stone cottage. When asked, the guide said that she was a mad old woman, dregs of the old days, sifted out from the mainstream of these great times. Two students from Beijing University intrigued by the ragged, dirty, grotesque jacket she wore, took their courage in both hands and went up to look at it more closely. On the left shoulder there was a shield-shaped blue epaulette; it was a foreign army jacket. These two students, interested in military science, became locked in debate over which country it came from: I think it looks like the uniform of the Indian army. Have you seen anything like it amongst the stuff you've read about Indian army uniforms? It looks like the uniform of American tank forces. Well! Have American armies ever been to Tibet? It must be a British uniform, then. You've hit the nail on the head.

Which of the armed services, then? At least a style common during the Second World War. Think, when did the British armies invade Tibet? I don't know. Let me tell you then, sorry, I don't know either. Look at the number "5" under the letter "A", what does it mean? That's simple. Army A, Division 5. Who was the general of Army A? You want to know about that? Let me tell you, but I am sorry I don't know either. How come this old woman is wearing it? That was a hard question for both of them. Finally they were unanimous in their conclusion: This old woman must have been the mistress of a white man in Division 5 of Army A. It was too dirty, disgustingly dirty, or it could have gone into their collection. They left, mumbling to each other all the way.

When quietness prevailed in Gokam again, Cering Gyamo, with the help of a cane, walked up to the rock which was covered with the scribbling of thousands of visitors. Fortunately the cave, hidden behind the entanglement of wild grass and vines, had not been discovered. Everytime there were visitors, she would sit on the threshold, watching their movements with her heart in her mouth. Once a rash lad had bumped into the small cave and, mistaking it for a pigeon's hold or a bird's nest, had thrust his hand inside for an egg. Hardly had he put in his fingers than he drew them out again as if electrified. Shaking his hand, he looked around with terrified eyes and left the cave perplexed. Cering Gyamo put her ear to the edge of the cave but there wasn't a sound. However, she did not have the slightest doubt that the great sangha was secluded in the cave. She put out her hands and felt the unintelligible marks which were to her like mysterious incantations: "Signed by Chungta, from the Farming and Stockbreeding Division of Shigatse Prefectural Committee"; "Huang Xiaoying, from the General Office of the Autonomous Region, signed Oct. 8, 1973"; "Learn from the Bangdui people"; "Wu Weihong, from Beijing, has visited this place"; "Han Jinle from Sichuan"; "From Lhasa ..." etc. She fetched a battered old brass ladle and scooped the clean water from the reservoir and spread it over the rock, believing that, by so doing, she could wash all the ominous things off the rock.

"Old Apa, don't be angry. Oh, please, don't pull the trigger, or you will be punished by law. Listen to me. I am a member of the UFO Association of China. This is my certificate, you see? This is an authentic certificate, there is no doubt about it. You scare me to death. I say, please don't point your gun at me in case it goes off accident. I am going. All right, I am going at once. But don't shoot me from behind. Damn it, there is nothing I can do to make him understand me. I am going anyway. I say, old Apa, don't think I am involved in any sabotage. As a matter of fact, I am writing a thesis. He doesn't understand me. I am asking to stay here for only one hour, no more. Just one hour, not a minute longer. I'll go at once the moment I find something here. You don't know what a great resemblance there is between this place and Nazca. I hope I can prove that astronauts from outer space landed at this very spot in ancient times. Ah, what is this? A rock. A rock. Ah, wonderful! Please, old Apa. I want nothing but this rock. Don't kill me. Please! Please!" The student, with a pair of glasses on his nose and a travelling bag on his back, as a last resort, went down on his knees all the while kowtowing to the old man who was holding the gun with his finger on the trigger, while his trembling hand crept over to the bright transparent rock. He knew that this herdsman, who did not understand a single word of Chinese, ignorant of law, let alone what UFO meant, could kill him any minute at the slightest whim.

"What are you up to here? If you are travelling past this place, I'll treat you as a guest, but you have your eyes glued to the ground, obviously trying to look for something. This won't do. I won't allow you to defile this place with your witchcraft. Don't take anything with you, not even a blade of grass." The old man stepped forward and directed a kick at the young man. Bending down, he grabbed the rock out of the young man's hand and placed it on his own palm. This was an extraordinary rock, transparent, shiny and glittering with soft light. What was more, contained in it were some odd signs and patterns. He had spent a greater half of his life here without seeing this rock, but it was discovered by this child who had been here for no more than half an hour. There must be something about him. As the rock belonged to this place, it ought to remain here forever and there was no taking it away. Before the student had time to stop him, the old man swung his arm round and threw the rock towards the lake. It fell into the water with a plop, sending up a splash of water which rippled out towards the bank.

"How stupid you are!" Heartbroken, the young man stretched out his arms and uttered a bitter cry. Beating his chest with his fists and stamping his feet on the ground, he burst into tears squatting on the ground with his head in his arms. Confronted with the desperate young man, the old herdsman was at a loss what to do.

"Is it the incarnation of your father? Or have you come to search for some spirit?" The old man bent forward to shake the delirious young man.

The student opened his blurry eyes, nodding and then shaking his head in confusion, stood up slowly and staggered away like a drunkard, his travelling bag in his hand.

"Stop and listen to me." The old man caught up with him. "What on earth is this rock? Were you trying to reveal some secret to me about this rock? Yes, you were, weren't you?"

Taking no notice of the old man, he went forward, his blank eyes staring far ahead.

"Come back, child. Come back!" the old man shouted at the top of his voice. He raised his gun and fired, the bullets flying over the young man's head. As if unconscious of the firing, he walked slowly off the edge of the plain.

The old man sat on the grass, dejected, holding his gun in his hands. Looking at the water in the lake with expressionless eyes, he suddenly thought he had done something silly. That bespectacled man must have known some secret about Mount Zela — a mystery he had been wanting to solve but did not know how. This mystery must have had something to do with the hardships he had gone through. Among the variety of people he had had contact with in one way or another in the course of his long lifetime — the woman he had picked up, the children he had raised, the young

merchant he had rescued, the Liberation Army men he
had received and the people he had run into down the
mountain — men, women, peasants, lamas, beggars,
lords, craftsmen and artists, he was more impressed by
far by the young man, or rather the indignation with
which he had walked away. Should he come back
some day, he thought, he would receive him as a
saint. He would allow him complete freedom to look
for anything he wanted because, he believed, the student would one day be able to help him solve the mystery he had kept at the bottom of his heart for so
long. For instance, why was he abandoned by his parents not long after he came into this world? Why had
he failed to get the woman for whom all his life he had
cherished the strongest desire? What was the thing that
had propelled him to come to this enormous plain and
keep the family-line going? Was the world he lived in
real? Did it belong to him? Was there, beyond the
mountains, another world more familiar and real to
him?

He began to pray in silence.

For three days running, there was no smoke curling
up from Gokam. Viewed from the stream that flowed
between the plain and the snow-clad peak, the reservoir
was like a shallow pit, without water. The miraculously-
constructed project had fallen into disuse. The water
from the snow-clad mountain streamed past the reservoir and, as usual, ran off the cliff down to the deep
pool and spread out through the sand dunes before it
flowed into the river. The colour of the stone cottage,
nestling in Gokam, was indistinguishable from the col-
ours of the surrounding canyons. During the years
Dalang lived on top of the plain, he hadn't passed a

single day without coming to the bank of the stream to stare in the direction of Gokam. When he was young and strong, he had made the journey on foot, but now, he rode an old dark brown horse, dozing off on its back all the way.

Putting his thumb and index finger into his mouth, Dalang gathered all his strength to blow a prolonged whistle towards the tent in the middle of the plain. The exhalation of air made him feel dizzy and exhausted, his eyes sparkling with little stars. His fifteen-year-old grand grandson who, in his childhood, had had one of his legs broken by the weight of an ewe, came galloping towards him on a white horse. Dalang told him to go down the mountain and tell the people there that they should come up to Gokam to see its last lonely villager. And he himself walked, using a cane, towards the edge of the cliff.

"Grandpa, it's dangerous!"

"Nonsense! I have walked this path before." Dalang glared at the boy, pugnaciously.

Ah, this is the very path I climbed when I came up here the first time. How long did I climb? I don't remember. It was already dark when I reached the top and I slept the night through against that rock up there. When I woke up the next morning, Good Heavens, where on earth was I? As if I were the only person in the world. Yes, I remember, I stepped on this rock and reached out my hands to hold to that small tree there. It is dead now. Just as everything lives, everything dies. The goats from Gokam have never set foot in such a dangerous place. No matter how hard I urged them, they wouldn't move, as if their feet had taken root in the rocks. I was really strong then. Oh, A false step. My Bodhisattva, come quick and save me! Dalang was hanging upside down, his feet off the rock. He saw the stream in Gokam flash past like a length of white thread and the surrounding mountains spinning around. He drifted down, down, unable to grasp at anything. He held fast to one thing, which went down with him, weightless, it was the cane in his hand. His heart went up to his throat, his chest and belly devoid of all organs. Ah, is this how you feel when flying? When you take your feet off the earth, you can hardly live. You don't know whether you are flying up or flying down. You spin and turn somersaults in midair. The most agonizing thing in the world is not how to live or how to die, but being forced to keep your body away from anything tangible. It is like wandering in hell. However, Cering Gyamo and I were predestined in our previous lives, as I was eventually granted the chance to see her again. But what about the most important wish of mine? Was I not expecting the bespectacled young man to come up to Mount Zela again?

Cering Gyamo lay on the low leather mattress, her hands propping up her chin, luring Dalang over with affectionate glances out of the corner of her eyes. Though the lamp light was dim, Dalang could still see the desire burning in her eyes. Her clothes unkempt and her waist belt undone; she turned over on the mattress flirtatiously, humming tunes in a light voice. She kept singing, without saying anything. Occasionally, she threw an agonized and affectionate look at Dalang.

"I am now the only one in Gokam," said Cering Gyamo.

"Besides me," Dalang responded.

"You? You have been fooling around outside."

"No. I have always wanted to marry you."

"You can marry me now." Cering Gyamo got up to shut the door, showing her bare breasts.

Dalang began to kick the door, shouting, "Hey! We are here to see the prospective bride with the dowry. Why are you closing the door when we have come all the way and are dying of thirst? Is it because you are reluctant to marry off your daughter at the last minute or because you think the dowry is too small?"

"Who is making such a nasty noise out there like a beggar?" Cering Gyamo asked from within. "If you damage this wooden door, I won't agree even if you offer to replace it with a gold one." So saying, she opened the door.

"Who is this ugly fellow? Look at your dirty ragged clothes. Where are the others who have come to see the bride with the dowry?"

After a bout of teasing each other with rough humour, the wedding ceremony was over. Then they shut the door again and sat on the mattress nestling against each other. At this happy moment, Cering Gyamo brought a pot of tea, two bowls of newly ground *tsamba*, two bowls of fresh butter and a sacrificial box with green barley in it, which they offered to the statue of Buddha while bowing three times and praying in chorus: "The Buddha, may we stay in love, devotion and safety all our lives." Having finished the prayer, Cering Gyamo stood up and, with a shrug of her shoulders, her clothes fell to the floor. Dalang immediately stretched out his rough hands, with one thousand ideas turning topsy-turvy in his head…. Am I a man? Come back, my lost soul. It's true that the slender grass tips can hurt the tender skin. Although Mount Zela hasn't made its sagacity felt, it is sagacious. Can you feel the eternal beauty and the rough softness of this plateau? Have you seen the lamb that has come out from between the rocks and wandered away from the flock of sheep? Can you see the lonely old cow standing on the grassy hillside, waiting for its death, but without complaint? Have you noticed the wind that has risen from nowhere? And the people who quietly come and go in the canyons and on the plain? The old herdsman sitting on the rock is looking towards the quiet rolling mountains, the high and mysterious blue sky and the air that fills everything in the universe, measuring in silence the height between heaven and earth; he is smelling the fragrance drifting from the valley, while listening to the silence of nature. He is thinking hard which stratum of space he is in, looking for his soul that has long gone out of his body; he is listening to the song, one that he has conceived over the years and has now become voiceless and will be buried forever at the bottom of his heart. But do you hear that the whole valley is rumbling with echoes?

Dalang's great-grandson had collected together a group of people from the foot of the mountain. Because of his crippled leg, instead of coming to Gokam, he went back home via Bangdui. One of the people he had brought was Tashi Dawa who still lived at the foot of the mountain. His legendary stories were long forgotten and, like any ordinary peasant of today, he lived with his wife and children. His eldest daughter, married, had one lovely chubby boy. He and his wife had seven *mu* of land and their two sons were running a transport business with the tractor they had bought. Two peasants had come with him to Gokam and, as ever, they adored Tashi Dawa. The last that came with him was a twenty-four-year-old girl, carrying a medical kit over her shoulder. Her father was one of the few high-ranking officials in the Tibetan government and he often made appearances on television. She had come with a research group sent by the Ministry of Public Health of the Central Government, to the Pagbug region to carry out a general survey of altitude sickness. On the way to Gokam, she had been calculating when the survey would be completed because very soon she would be going to the United States to study medicine at a medical college in California and she needed time to improve her English. She was determined to be the first Tibetan woman to attain, in the next few years, a doctorate degree in medicine awarded by a foreign university.

Cering Gyamo lay on the leather mattress serenely, her eyes two slits hardly distinguishable from the wrinkles on her face, and her head covered with sparse bristles, black and shiny. She still had on the old-fashioned jacket of the British Royal Engineers, colour faded, the cuffs and the lower edges of the front worn to a fringe of threads, and a pair of home-made woollen socks with the toes sticking out. The lamp was still flickering with the last few drops of oil, as if trying to keep going until somebody came on the scene before she passed away. Beside her there was an earthenware pot filled with butter tea and a leather bag filled with *tsamba*. The butter tea had turned cold, with a layer of cream on top. No one knew why the tea and *tsamba* had been prepared. She must have thought of leaving this place before she died, the peasants from the foot of the mountain guessed.

"I thought she was ill," the young woman doctor sighed. She left the stale room and looked around Gokam with curiosity. Although the dam was dilapidated, the irrigation ditch and the water gate broken, it still had some air that suggested how spectacular it must have looked in the old days.

The peasants took down the door and carried her out on it. They didn't understand why Tashi Dawa insisted that she be carried down the mountain.

"Wait a minute," the doctor came over and, taking a look at Cering Gyamo's face, put out a finger and pressed her face that had lost all elasticity. "Do we need a postmortem examination?"

"No," Tashi Dawa said.

"Better not let people see her face." He produced a white handkerchief and spread it over her face. "You can go ahead. I've got blisters on my feet. Don't worry about me. I'll catch up."

They carried Cering Gyamo down the mountain, leaving the brave girl behind at Gokam alone.

She scarcely knew what she was looking for when she came across a small path covered by dry grass. She stepped over the narrow stream, kicked the broken rocks off the path and walked up to the huge rock intersecting the road. There was nothing on the rock except for the inscriptions cut by the visitors. When she rapped at it with her knuckles, it produced a hollow sound. When she rapped a second time, there was a cracking sound. When she rapped the third time, a stone slab fell to the ground and broke in pieces, hurting the backs of her feet. "Ah!" She cried lightly. In front of her there was a very narrow cave in which a whitish skeleton sat on a knee-high earthen altar as if in meditation, with the right hand bent on the right pelvis and the left hand resting on the left thigh — a very rare sitting position of Bodhisattva. The skeleton, already fossilized, had become one with the rocky wall, like a figure in relief. Under the skeleton there was a layer of dry grass with a rusty bronze pestle beside it, and a wooden bowl and two or three old bronze statues. On the wall behind the skeleton, there were many hand and foot marks.

Standing in front of the skeleton, the young doctor appreciated it as if it were a work of art. According to her rough assessment, the skeleton was of a man, who had died a long long time ago, aged twenty-four or twenty-five. She was regretting that she could not take it back to the hospital for a specimen when she heard a rustle behind her and she looked back.

A Buddhist rosary fell from nowhere. It didn't break. She picked it up, looking around.

"Cering Gyamo." A voice rang in her ears.

"Yes!" she answered, her legs going weak. She saw an old man sitting in the place where the skeleton had been. She didn't know which was real, the skeleton or the old man.

"I know that Gokam will never be deserted. There will always be people living here." The old man sat tilting against the rocky wall, listless.

"I, I am not...."

"Cering Gyamo, count and see how many beads there are on the string." The old man gestured to her.

"One hundred and eight," she blurted out, not

knowing what she was saying.

"Every one of the beads is a period of time. Every one of them is a Cering Gyamo and Cering Gyamo is every woman." The old man opened his eyes, considering her seriously for a long while. Finally he came out with the truth that had never been made known to human beings before.

Miracles take place every minute, but there is only one river of time that flows with eternal history and the thousands of men and women....

Translated by Liu Shicong

Plateau Serenade

"HEY! Give us a song ... what's your name?" Norzhol asked, turning on the light in the driver's cab. Beside him sat the girl from the grasslands who had just asked him for a lift.

"Nini," she replied, raising her head slightly.

" ... Nini? Hey, how about a song, whatever you like. It'll keep us awake, otherwise we'll never reach Lhasa going round the plateau like this in endless circles," Norzhol warned drowsily.

Nini withdrew her curious gaze and looking around, started to sing. Her voice was so loud that it drowned out the roar of the engine.

> *Hey! The sun has set behind the snowy mountain,*
> *Cattle and sheep have been driven into the pen.*
> *Girls with water barrels on their backs*
> *Are walking towards the winding river bank....*

For a while Norzhol did not speak. "Is that what you call singing?" he complained. "Do you think I'm deaf?"

"I'm not shouting, I'm singing," she muttered.

"Hey, girl, do you know what pop songs are sung in Lhasa now?" Norzhol said and began to croon a vivid imitation of a popular song.

"I meet you by chance, you and me.... I have a little cough and an itching throat. You get the idea? It's

the modern way of singing. Wow, you country bumpkin, I simply can't believe that you've never been to
Lhasa."

"What! What did you say?"

"Oh, I just said — what a pity you've never been
to Lhasa. Just now you asked me what people in
Lhasa are like. Look at me, then you'll know."
Norzhol produced a pair of sunglasses from his
jacket pocket and was about to put them on when
he remembered that their dark lenses would totally ob-
scure his vision.

"Look at me carefully," he said, staring straight
ahead, one hand on the steering wheel, the other holding open his leather coat to reveal his manly figure.
"Japanese hairstyle. Seen the Japanese film *Close Pur-
suit*?... No! What a pity. See my shirt? Tartan with a
pointed collar, the latest fashion. And check out these,
genuine jeans, not bell-bottoms."

"Ah, so that's what Lhasa people are like," Nini
said naively. "Lhasa must be an unsafe place, then?"

"Who told you that? What do you mean by
'unsafe'?"

Nini thought for a while, then replied, "Eh.... There
must be many men there."

"Rubbish! What do you know? How could there
possibly be a world without men? Where are you
going to stay?"

"I've got a relative. He's a carpenter."

"Why didn't you start out a few days earlier? Everyone in Lhasa is drinking and dancing. Tomorrow's
New Year. Right now, the only people on this god-
damned grassland are us. A corner forsaken by love."

"A what?" Nini couldn't quite catch his words.

"Nothing. It's something written in a novel," Norzhol said vaguely.

Nini told him that she and her mother lived on a remote grassland. This year, seeing as they had been allocated quite a lot of money, she had decided to go to Lhasa to have a look round, but had lost her way. Then she asked, "Why didn't you stay in Lhasa to celebrate New Year?"

Norzhol held the steering wheel absent-mindedly and went on about how all the offices in the bureau had run out of cow-dung for fuel. As none of the married drivers was willing to spend New Year in the wilderness, the job had naturally fallen to the young unmarried ones. Finally, he declared piously, "If I'd remained in Lhasa celebrating the New Year, you would have had to wait for days before seeing another truck. And look at the snow, you would have been dead long ago."

Nini opened her mouth and stuck out her pink tongue to express her good fortune and gratitude. Norzhol noticed that her eyes, like a pair of chattering stars, never left his face. Her bold, curious gaze reminded him of the story of the creation of Man, told by a Han friend: Adam woke up in the garden and found Eve staring at him, the first man, surprise in her limpid eyes. The truck bumped over a pot hole, swaying from left to right. Nini rolled into Norzhol's arms like a funny fat panda. Clumsily she quickly righted herself. "You are a joke. I expect you haven't even ridden a bus before, have you?" Norzhol sniggered.

"Yes ... ah!" Before she could reply, Nini rolled into Norzhol's arms for the second time. She was angry, "Why can't I sit properly?"

"You should hold onto the handrail ... it's there," Norzhol laughed, unable to support himself. His body swayed with the jolting of the truck and a voice began to ring in his head, "A bite tells you whether a peach is sour; a kiss tells you whether a girl loves you." Who had sung it?... Oh yeah, the driver of the bureau's Beijing jeep. The fragments of song would linger around the whole day long. "The most fragrant on the grassland is butter; the sweetest is the lips of a girl." Perhaps there was some truth in it. They grow up drinking milk after all. Why not have a try, it doesn't matter since we're the generation of the '80s. My head is as hard as bronze, girls' hands are as soft as silk. They wouldn't hurt ... go on....

The headlights shone through the swirling snowflakes onto a small ditch ahead. He calculated the distance. As the front wheels of the truck lurched over the ditch, Norzhol turned and rapidly planted a firm kiss on Nini's red lips as precisely as he had bitten into that ripe peach hanging from the tree in his childhood. He tasted something sweet, knowing that Nini would react the way the girls in Lhasa did: scream, spit a stream of curses, or even shake her fist.

Not a sound. Norzhol cast Nini a glance. She was lost in thought, her cheeks burning crimson; her wide-open vacant eyes, flashed with a strange light as if she were intoxicated.

Disturbed by Nini's silence, Norzhol felt uneasy and asked irritably, "Are you dumb?"

For a while, Nini did not reply.

"Why did you touch my lips?" she asked, looking up.

"Ha.... So that's how it is. You should be more

open-minded, you stupid girl.''

"My mother will cry if she knows. You shouldn't have treated me like that.... Stop.''

Baffled, Norzhol brought the truck to a halt. Nini picked up her bundle from under her seat, got out and climbed into the back of the truck.

"Hey, what are you doing?'' Norzhol followed her out.

Nini stood there, her chest rising and falling in agitation. Within moments her shoulders were covered with a layer of snow. She licked her lips as if to remove the snowflakes on them. "My mother has told me countless times not to allow men to touch me,'' Nini stammered, "I cannot share a seat with you.''

"It's the driver's cab,'' Norzhol corrected.

"I'm afraid.''

Scowling, Norzhol pleaded and promised not to touch her again. "Nini, listen to me. Get down quickly, I beg you, or you'll be frozen to death.''

Nini gave him an odd look. Slowly she crouched down as if she were about to tumble out, then straightened up abruptly. "No! No!'' she shouted.

"All right,'' Norzhol took off his leather coat and, panting with rage, flung it up to her. "You can go higher up if you want to appreciate the night, you can sing loud enough to wake up the whole world. You've got a whole truckload of dry cow-dung all to yourself. Eat it if you're hungry, free of charge. And remember, don't blow up your stomach.''

Ahead was a rough stretch of unpaved road and the truck swayed like a drunkard. Norzhol drove, harbouring his grievances. He glanced at his watch, it was already 2:40. Outside, the bitter wind swept past, flinging up wet snow onto the windscreen. The temperature had fallen to thirty degrees below zero and the heat discharged by the engine was of no use whatsoever.

Norzhol's fingers stiffened with cold and he shivered all over. Worried about Nini, he brought the truck to a halt, opened the door and began to climb up the back. "Come down quickly, Nini," he shouted. "We are running into an icy current, you'll freeze to death!"

The minute he poked his head up over the edge, he was assailed by a volley of dry cow-dung which hit his nose so hard that it brought tears to his eyes. "Hey," Nini shouted back, "don't come near, don't touch me, or I'll hit you!" She was as fierce as a lion.

Norzhol yelled as he continued on up, "Nini, I'm doing this for you, but all you do is feed me cow-dung. Come down quickly. This is my vehicle, you've got to listen to me."

"Down! Down!" Nini pushed him furiously.

"You country bumpkin! You wait, I'll smash you to pieces! You'd better count how many bones you have first."

Nini went berserk. She untied the "ererdou"* from her waist and with a scream, lashed out at Norzhol as if she were punishing a troublesome yak. Each whip lash was as precise and vigorous as his kiss. He fell to the snow-covered ground and lay there for a while with

---

*"Ererdou" is a whip used to herd sheep. At either end is a length of rope; the middle part consists of a leather pouch containing a pebble which is catapulted at a target.

his head in his hands, then leapt up and dashed into the cab like an enraged lion. He accelerated as hard as he could, and with a howl the truck rushed forward angrily along the faintly visible road.

"Bang! Bang! Bang!" Nini struck the top of the driver's cab violently, her shrill cries mingling with a barrage of other sounds.

"Go on, hit it as hard as you can. Freezing to death is just what you deserve, and if you fall off and die, it'll serve you right, too. Let the wolf have your bones!" Norzhol roared, his face distorted with rage, his body shaking all over. He seemed to see Nini's frightened eyes and her desperation: Hands stretched out, she was crying helplessly; the whole load of cow-dung had swept over her like a huge wave; except for her pale hands, she was completely buried. The truck came to a sharp turn. Norzhol swung the wheel vehemently without applying the brakes. The truck swerved, then whistled past a boulder, shuddering as if it were about to explode. Norzhol was tossed up and down like a ball....

The storm continued. The truck lurched madly.

He didn't know how much time had elapsed by the time the truck had calmed down and his anger had been cooled by the icy snow. The truck came to the end of the rough road and turned onto the smooth asphalt surface. The storm had stopped unnoticed and the white blanket of the plain radiated a crystal light. For quite some time, his mind was blank and he could not remember what had happened, feeling nothing but his own existence in the world such as he had experienced countless times before when he was all alone on those return journeys to Lhasa. Severe loss of sleep had completely dehydrated him. He was like a dried-up goat. His blood was cold as if solidified; the skin of his face was unbearably taut and his mouth bitter and puckered. He was in a trance, unconscious of whether he was driving the truck or the truck was carrying him. They were like two fatigued companions dragging each other along the road.

Norzhol suddenly woke up from this drowsy state and his mind began to function normally. He turned off the engine and dashed out, shouting, "Nini! Nini!"

A sudden silence descended which filled his heart with emptiness and despair. Dead, everything dead. "Maybe I just had a dream. No one asked for a lift. There's only me, Norzhol, in this truck __ its owner and its slave! No, there's Nini! And her fearful voice, her charming eyes and her ferocious attack...."

"Nini! Where are you? Are you still alive?" Norzhol called out anxiously and clambered up the back. He saw nothing but black cow-dung. Overcome with anxiety, he almost cried. Suddenly he saw something wriggle under the petrol tank. He went forward, regardless of any impropriety. Nini, wrapped tightly in the greasy leather coat, huddled in a corner, half her body buried in the cow-dung.

"Nini, are you still alive?"

In the chilly moonlight, Nini's eyes twinkled. She wanted to speak, but couldn't. "Damn, damn!" Norzhol cursed himself as he pulled Nini out of the cow-dung. He carried her off the truck, but didn't know where to put her. He circled the snowy ground like a leopard in search of a safe cave, carrying its cub in its mouth. Finally he dashed towards a slope.

Setting her down, he quickly fetched a large pile of cow-dung and lit the blowlamp. Waves of warmth, flames, and moving figures. Soon the night was permeated with life and animation.

"I'm ... cold," Nini uttered feebly. Norzhol jumped over and took her in his arms. He was worried his strong arms might crush her to pieces. "Hurt?" he asked.

Nini trembled. She shook her head, her brows knitted. "Cold! Hold me tighter!" she moaned weakly.

Norzhol tightened his hold. "I'm almost frozen to death," Nini groaned in contentment and buried her head deep in his arms. Her skin shone in the light of the fire like a new rose bud.

An hour passed. Nini slowly regained her strength. She raised her head and looked at Norzhol animatedly. The smile in the corner of her mouth was like the moon sliding out from behind the clouds. She licked her finger and wiped the traces of blood off Norzhol's neck. "Forgive me," she uttered softly, "I hit you too hard. I have never used such strength before. Really, I don't know why.... We country folk are not equal to you people from Lhasa. My mother told me not to allow men to touch me. I've got to listen to her," she said, crying. "Ah, you are so strong. No one has ever held me so tightly.... You're so kind. I hit you too hard," she said and sighed with relief.

"No, I'm a disgrace to the Lhasa people. It's no more than I deserve. I've really been a fool. I should have protected you, poor Nini."

"We are both punished.... No! You are a good man, a modern man."

He didn't know since when Nini had carved this

new word in her mind.

"Huh! How can I be regarded as modern? Damn! What about you then?"

"A country bumpkin."

"No! Eve."

"Who is Eve?"

"The first woman."

The sky was studded with stars in the east. At the foot of a distant snowy mountain were a few dots of yellow starlight. Norzhol knew it was a highway maintenance squad. "You must be hungry," he said, "let's go and get some food."

Nini closed her eyes comfortably and said, "Let's sit for a little while longer."

Norzhol began to feel hot beside the flaming fire. He closed his aching eyes, considering whether he should release her. Suddenly, his forehead was touched by something soft and cool. Opening his eyes, he saw two lively stars sparkling in front of him. Nini took his head in her arms. "Now, we're good friends," she said and laughed, "Let's touch our foreheads together as blessings for both of us."

"Nini!"

......

The knocking on the door woke up the couple from the maintenance squad. A faint trace of moonlight glimmered outside the window. The table was littered with cups and plates. They must have had a very happy New Year. The man gave his wife a shove, "Hey! Wake up. It sounds like a truck on its way back to Lhasa. Maybe they want to stay."

The wife pulled on her clothes, went out for a while, then came back in, closed the door and slithered under the quilt again. "You're just lazy," the man mumbled.

"Pooh! Move in a bit. Don't you see it's snowing outside…. Phew! It's really cold."

"How many?"

"They've gone. They just had some food, a happy young couple. Don't know why they spent New Year on the road."

"To be out on New Year's Eve, they must have done something wicked. Go to sleep!"

Moments later, as they lay there drifting off, they heard the engine starting up.

The truck drove off towards Lhasa and once again the world was at peace.

Translated by Wang Ying

Over the River

THE river was as wide as a lake, a sea, or a plain. The village at the foot of distant mountains over the river would have seemed more illusory had it not been for a few green dots on the bank — lonely willow trees that brought the distant village nearer.

Water as smooth as brocade flowed with boundless dignity towards somewhere over the horizon.

The poor village on this side of the river had seventy-odd households, their shabby stone houses scattered along the slope. Yak dung cakes for fuel were drying on walls; roosters perched on the roofs crowing. A brook of meltwater from a nearby mountain wound its way through the village. At the entrance to the village was a huge pipal tree, probably planted by the first settler here. Villagers made occasional trips across the river to the co-op for a few daily goods: sugar, tea, white cotton, needles and thread.

Morning on the bank. A young man and a little girl were pushing a yak-skin raft into the water. He was her senior by more than ten years.

"Will you take me along, Brother Danzeng?" the girl demanded habitually, as she had done many times before.

"You're too young," he replied in the same manner. Besides, she had to tend the goats.

"What's the village across the river like? Is it big?"

"Yeah."

"Do they have headscarves in the co-op?"

"Yeah."

"Brother Danzeng?"

"What?"

"Will you bring me a green one?"

"Yes."

"Don't forget."

By then villagers had gathered on the shore, waiting to cross the river either to visit relatives or barter.

The raft was sliding away.

The little girl was still shouting, her foot in the water.

Danzeng smiled, his muscular arms and chest plying the oars strenuously — the very picture of a dauntless raftsman.

Swinging a branch, the girl slowly drove her goats up the barren hill, from where the raft seemed no bigger than a beetle. She waved to it, then sat down on a stone to muse on the green scarf — it would be eye-catching in these drab parts.

She was a lonely, quiet shepherdess, who had been orphaned when she was very young and brought up by a one-eyed old storekeeper. Like the other girls in the village, she had spent her sixteen years among livestock.

Danzeng was an orphan too, and probably for this reason he treated her like an elder brother. She often rested her chin on his knees in the evening inside his low, shabby hut by the river, and listened to the same monotonous and age-old story by the dim castor-oil light:

" ... Fairy Lamu waited and waited in the forest, until one sunny day he arrived in a red cloak on a white steed — "

She would soon fall asleep. At midnight he would gently carry her back to the store.

The villagers had to rush their suppers in the those days, for at the sound of the summoning gong, they would gather in a big, smoke-filled room to listen to the Party secretary dwell on politics deep into the night, their backs and legs aching from a day's labour.

The little girl would pillow her head on his shoulder and sleep, and when they were dismissed, he would take her to the store.

Life in the village was as monotonous as Danzeng's story and as tedious as the meetings, punctuated only by love and youth. Young people sometimes hid in haystacks or fields for fun, or dallied in the sunshine....

They held the young raftsman by the arm, asking, "When will you have a gentle girl serve you buttered tea in your low hut?"

"My girl is too young, like an unfledged bird," he would answer.

But who is she? And when will my sweetheart be fledged?

Before the raftsman was even aware, his sweetheart's eyes had begun to shine, her breasts to swell and her complexion to become ruddy. One day the storekeeper brought his raft from across the river. He was excited; the pocket of his yak-wool sweater bulged and his eyes were glazed with drink.

"Great! Everything is set." The old man laughed heartily.

"I haven't seen you so happy for ages, uncle."

"It's a good family. All able-bodied. And they want to marry Dolma. Even I can move in with them.

What else could I want?"

"Dolma is going to marry?"

"Yes, of course — Why's this raft going round?"

She cried for no reason the day she married, doing exactly as girls were required to on such an occasion. However, when she had done, her face revealed her excitement, for across the river was her holy place. She had lived seventeen years, long enough, in this poor village, and best of all, the one-eyed old man had found her an affluent family.

Probably he should have taken her to have a look across the river, the young raftsman thought, and now she was leaving forever.

She was not the only girl taking his raft to marry across the river. They had had several that year. And each time a girl married across the river, lads from the village would stand under the pipal tree in twos and threes hopelessly looking at the departing raft, their eyes dark with melancholy.

They worked hard, but the village girls married across river. Why?

Although she was getting married, everything about her was simple, except for a new dress, the first she had ever had, and a *hada* attached to the raft. She and the one-eyed old man were the only passengers, and had their few belongings with them.

Nevertheless the green headscarf the young raftsman had given her a year before was still on her head, and still bright green.

She hummed as she played with the water. She was very innocent.

"Brother Danzeng," she asked, "what are those

things that shine at night across the river? Are they electric lights?''

"Yeah.''

"Do they hang inside rooms?''

"Yeah.''

"Is it true that you can see a needle on the ground by them?''

"You button your lip!'' the raftsman flared, his face distorted, grinding his teeth.

The one-eyed old man cast him a knowing glance.

She was scared. She couldn't work out why he was behaving so. She was very innocent.

When they drew alongside, several strangers were waiting on the otherwise deserted wharf to pick up the girl and the old man in a wagon. They had several miles to go, to a village over a ridge. With a crack of the whip, the wagon started, its wheels creaking in the sand, and now she cried, this time in earnest. She pulled the green scarf off her head and said between sobs, "Come and see me whenever you can, Brother Danzeng, please!''

The young raftsman remained by the willows, leaning on his oars. He shook his head and narrowed his eyes in agony.

"Don't forget.'' Her voice was as faint as a breeze.

After that he avoided the village. Whenever he went across the river he glanced sidelong at the distant ridge, then hoisted his gear on his back and walked upstream, leaving footprints in the sand, some deep, some shallow, so as to row back downstream.

One day several months later he found her waiting for him on the wharf.

"You're hateful," she accused him. "You never come to see me." Her hair danced in disarray before her face, her dress was untidy, and the green scarf was gone.

"You're his, each hair of your head. I can't come."

"But he's a drunkard, and he beats me dreadfully."

"The bastard!" he cursed between his teeth.

"Why didn't you marry me?" she murmured.

"Do I have livestock and money? Under these worn-out clothes there's only my skin." His lips tightened when he saw the passengers all aboard.

She drew from her bosom some soft, yellow butter wrapped in lettuce leaves and gave it to him. "You don't have much of this over there, and you're getting thin."

"Don't come again, Dolma."

"How I wish I could go back," she sighed.

She never again came to the bank.

When the villagers no longer had to labour on infertile mountain slopes two years later, they resumed their age-old trades of making exquisite pottery and collecting mushrooms and medicinal herbs in the scrub. Along with the booming handicraft industry and sideline production came more hustle and bustle in the village.

Young lovers gathered under the pipal tree at night and by the light of a bonfire danced the age-old *duixie* dance, which had long sunk into oblivion.

This was no longer a poor place.

The young raftsman shipped local products across

the river every day and returned with ever more
dazzling household goods. He often sat on the shore
lost in thought, his eyes on the glimmering lights
across the river. The dark water seemed congealed
and stagnant but for the ripples whirling by the
bank. They were the only sign of life and motion.
He sat there in the pale moonlight, accompanied by his
shadow.

Was anyone telling her a story? And where was she
now?

Someone across the river said she had left for the
county town on training leave, and that before she left
she had sat alone by the willows all night long, holding her knees. Only the young raftsman knew the
reason.

Another two years passed. As life got better his raft
was replaced by a motor-boat. One winter's day he
was shipping pottery packed in hay, and mushrooms
and medicinal herbs in sacks. Ice at the bow broke
into pieces, stood on end along the sides of the boat
and were tossed away by the churning water at the
stern.

Dolma waited in a composed manner on a tractor,
her eyes on the approaching boat.

They were alone at the wharf. They studied each
other like strangers.

"You can handle tractors. Why is your hair so
untidy?" he asked.

"And you've got a motor-boat," she replied.
"Why is your beard so long?"

Their breath froze at their mouths. Both managed a
bitter, dry smile.

"Let's get to work," she urged, raising her hands

to her mouth for warmth. Neither of them spoke during the work. They felt they had so much to say and had said it all.

They often met in this way from then on.

As the weather got warmer the willows put out buds and new leaves. One morning early in summer the young man found no tractor at the wharf. He looked across the wilderness, seeing nothing except for some trees gently waving in the breeze.

He unloaded the cargo, which he stacked neatly on the ground, then sat down and began to scrawl with a branch. Dolma, Dolma, Dolma — nothing else on the golden sand but her name.

She appeared beyond the ridge like a drunkard, sand on her face and her dress torn open at the shoulder.

"The tractor turned over." She paused to get her breath a while, before heading for the water to wash her face.

He jumped up and followed her hurriedly to the scene of the accident, repair kit in hand.

Goats moved about far away on the mountainside. Their bleating could be heard. Where was the goatherd?

When he skirted the ridge he saw the tractor lying on its side in the sand like an injured bull, sacks scattered everywhere. He disengaged the tractor from the trailer and with the girl's help raised the tractor on to its wheels. Dolma started the engine. Nothing was wrong, except that the tank was empty. While the girl went to the river for water, Danzeng reloaded the tractor.

Both were exhausted when the work two hours later

was done. He lay half asleep on the sand. A mysterious fragrant breeze rose. The girl knelt by him and wiped away his sweat with her green scarf. He fixed his eyes on the scarf, which, though faded and mended, was still bright against the drab sand.

"You should have got a new one long ago," he said, looking away.

"He gave me one, but I lost it."

"You're lying."

"No, you know nothing about it."

His chest began to heave. He held Dolma's shoulders, turned her around and said passionately, "Listen, you have ruined me."

"No. Don't be like this. We're not alone."

She jumped up, smoothed her hair and said, "Let's get going. We're behind time."

He sat beside her as she skilfully manoeuvred the tractor along the bumpy road, their shoulders pressed against each other.

"How did you turn it over?" he asked.

"A pigeon was in the road. I didn't want to be late. No, I can't explain." Her anger suddenly rose. "What can I do? And I'm not to blame. You cared for me, so why didn't you say you wanted to marry me? And I was so innocent; all I wanted was to go and have a look at the co-op, the tractors and the electric lights. I came because all the other girls married across the river. You're callous! Callous! Callous!"

She turned around still sobbing and began to pound his chest.

"Look out!" he cried. The tractor almost turned over again.

Then a silence, during which he wondered to himself, "Am I to blame?"

She cast a sidelong glance at him, then handed him a towel from her neck. "Wipe your sweat."

He took the towel. It smelt of hay, gasoline and her warmth.

It was time to go, but neither of them wanted to be the first to start the engine.

"You go first," he urged her.

"No, you."

"No, you," he insisted. "Your family will be worried."

She opened her mouth but uttered no word. As her tractor throbbed she turned around and said dreamily with drooping eyelids, "He died of drink three years ago."

The tractor leaped forward like a drunkard.

He felt like crying but was choked by a lump in his throat. He felt like weeping, but no tears came. All he could do was wave shakily.

It was a gorgeous morning. There was no wind at all on the river. As his boat glided across with him at the tiller, his eyes strained to the far bank, and he murmured, "I'm coming for you, to marry you."

The tractor had long been waiting on the wharf. He jumped out of his boat impatiently before it was firmly moored, only to be greeted by a strange, pretty girl with an innocent face, who glanced at her watch and said, "She's gone. I came instead, and I've been waiting over two hours."

He stood there confused.

"What's the matter with you? Do you mind? She was taken to Lhasa by car."

"You're lying." He wouldn't believe her.

"I swear by my mother. Dolma is a model worker. Have you never travelled by car?"

"No." He shook his head.

"Neither have I. You seem to be in love with her. Someone's in love with me too."

"Did she say anything before she left?"

"No. Oh, yes. She said she wanted to go back to her home village."

Her home village. He narrowed his eyes and looked back. His village against the mountain across the river was no more than a white dot dancing slightly in the heat haze like something out of a fairy tale. It was her home village too.

"What a wide river!" the girl exclaimed, her eyes following his.

The age-old river flowed on under the scorching sun.

Translated by Li Quoqing

The Free Man Qimi

QIMI was walking along the muddy road to Luoda Town. The rough sand was very painful under his feet. From time to time, still walking, he would turn round and glance backwards as if enjoying the sight of the long, winding row of footprints he had left behind. Sometimes his head would bump against a tree-trunk as he faced forward again, or, before he was aware of it, he would run into other pedestrians, or stumble into the ditch along the road.

Now, there was only himself walking along the road.

The inhabitants of Luoda Town believed in the Goddess Boko. They would vow in pious and earnest tones, "In the name of Boko!"

Often, a policeman would appear at the corner of the square and, hands clasped behind his back, he would walk leisurely down the street.

Qimi entered the town and stopped at a grocery. On seeing him, people began to whisper to each other:
"It's the fifth time Qimi's escaped from prison."
"No, the eighth time."

This was the main street, on either side of which were several grocery shops, bars, a tailor's shop and a blacksmith's. People lived in the houses along the street.

Qimi nodded to his acquaintances, caring nothing that the attitude towards him was respectful yet distant.

Ngamao, the owner of the grocery, saw him and said, her hands over her chest, "Qimi, you're back again?"

"Yes, not bad, is it?"

"Oh!" She didn't know what to say next. "Winter's coming." After a while, she asked again, "They haven't set you free, have they?"

"No, I did it myself again."

He sat down on the threshold and accepted the snuffbottle Ngamao offered him. He put a little on the nail of his left thumb. Other traders began to greet him.

Qimi knew very well that he shouldn't return to Luoda each time he escaped, instead, he should run far away. However, he couldn't imagine where else he could go. To him, nowhere, except Luoda, could offer him the freedom of saying whatever he wanted and the intimacy when people called out to him.

"What?" said the shopkeeper in a low voice. "You'll be arrested again and taken back to prison before you've smoked a pouch of tobacco?"

"Which family is cooking mutton?" Qimi's nose detected the aroma. He never bothered about what the shopkeeper said.

"It's opposite Melung's. I saw him bring back a piece of mutton this morning. If he knows you've come back, I'm sure he'll invite you to dinner."

"That'll be good." He rubbed his hands against his lips.

Suddenly, all the people in the street turned to look north and then back at Qimi: a figure was appearing.

It was the policeman strolling down the street, hands behind his back. Qimi was hesitant. He stood up and craned his neck to get a look, only to find the police-man had already noticed him. Nervously, he raised his leg as though preparing to kick the door and run. But, his leg remained motionless in mid-air as the po-liceman nodded at him and passed by, then went on his way as if deep in thought about some riddle the answer to which had been puzzling him all his life.

Everyone felt relieved.

"Qimi, they're really released you this time?" ask-ed people.

"Anyway, I managed to get out in my own way."

Everyone started getting on with their own business.

After saying goodbye to Ngamao, Qimi went into a tea-house beside the square. Few customers were there. He tapped the empty cup and a girl came up to pour him some tea.

He sipped the tea.

He didn't bother to try and guess why they had set him free.

Opposite him was a young man, who was looking out of the window. His name was Jam Waje, the son of the town's well-known Jam family. People rarely saw him because it was said he was weak and constant-ly falling ill. So, because of his condition, he was kept inside the big house all day long. He appeared aloof and lonely, with melancholy yet beautiful eyes. Qimi knew him only slightly.

"Young master," Qimi nodded to him.

"So you're back."

"Yeah."

"How's everything?"

"Everything?"

"Everything."

"Fine. Boko blesses me."

Jam Waje nodded with satisfaction, then looked out of the window again. Outside was the street, where you could see the withered walnut tree at the far end. The people in the street were all from Luoda, and they all knew each other.

"What are you going to do?" demanded Jam Waje.

"I'll see."

"Why don't you take up your former profession?"

"I can't. Anyway, they won't let me. You know, my hands are only suitable for cleaning sacrificial utensils and bronze statues in lamaseries." Qimi showed the young man his hands.

The hands were rare and exquisite — incredible that they belonged to Qimi: the skin was smooth and delicate, lustrous and soft like cream, which, if even slightly touched, would leave a mark. The fine hairs on the back had dew-like moisture on them and, under the transparent skin, winding pale blue veins could easily be detected. Qimi enjoyed them complacently for a while before hiding them deep between his legs.

"You seem to be waiting for somebody," he said.

The other made no reply.

"Or for some miracle to happen," muttered Qimi. "A score and more of years tells me that you could have everything you ever dreamed about at night, but when you open your eyes, you realize that nothing miraculous exists, don't you?"

"All the time, I've been trying to understand the real value of those wooden bowls in my family. They must symbolize something. Perhaps an itinerant monk will disclose the truth to me."

"So have I. I have been besieged by the thought that the wooden bowls might be the incarnations of women."

"Women? Yes, wonderful! Go ahead."

"It's nonsense, young master."

"Nonsense or not, please go on."

"Have you ever heard this song? It goes like this: it's not convenient to take you with me, but I hate leaving you behind; if only you could change into a wooden bowl, I would put you close to my breast and go to the utmost ends of the earth."

"Oh, that's your explanation."

"It's just nonsense."

"Women."

"How many wooden bowls are there in your family now?" inquired Qimi.

From time immemorial, the Jam family had been feuding with another rich and powerful family, and they had drawn a border-line between their doors. Neither side was allowed to cross the line, a regulation observed for generations. Once, a drunk maidservant from the other family took the wrong door into the Jams' courtyard, and was raped by a groom of the Jams' in a pile of firewood behind the kitchen. At that time, there was no court of law, so, to solve the dispute, the two families sat on either side of the line, praying to Boko. They told her the details of the affair and begged her to have pity on them and give her unfortunate subjects a fair verdict. All the residents in the town came along to enjoy the spectacle. Some sat on walls, others in trees, and still others stood on rooftops. As they watched nervously, they dared not even breathe. The two families, with their eyes closed, waited for the coming of a miracle. Quietude reigned over the place. Before long, a clap of thunder sounded in the sky, but few dared to look up. It was said later that several brave youths had looked up but had been blinded immediately by an intensely bright, colourful ring of light and they couldn't even speak for a time. From the firmament came the verdict from the invisible Goddess: Jam Soitang (Waje's ancestor) would present a red-elm bowl to Purlo Gunsang Jepu (owner of the maidservant) as compensation.

No other god could give a fairer verdict, everyone was convinced.

From then on, whenever the Jams got into trouble, they would produce a suitable wooden bowl as compensation, and everyone sincerely believed in the goodwill of the gesture.

This was the legend passed down from generation to generation.

"Hit me on the head with your fist," said Qimi.

"Where?"

"My head. Knock me out."

"Want to get a wooden bowl?"

"To be frank, it's been my long-cherished wish."

"In that case, doesn't it mean that I give you the bowl for nothing?"

"You're right. Well, never mind."

"You should take up your former profession," said Jam Waje.

"I can't. I'm born to clean sacrificial utensils and bronze statues in lamaseries. I wonder why those lamas refuse to give me a tonsure and allow me to serve there."

"Why have they set you free?"

"I don't know. And what's the good of knowing the reason?"

"Anyway, from now on, you're a free man again."

"Right, I'm as free as the wind." As Qimi said the word "free", he felt he was as empty as the wind as well.

"Cheers!" Jam Waje said.

They drank up one glass and another was served.

Qimi had no money but he knew that the young man would pay for him. He had money and, as expected, was not in the least hesitant about doing so.

"What did you do before?" asked Jam Waje in a low voice.

"What, you really don't know?"

"No. Don't stare at me like that. Your eyes are like two walnuts."

"In the name of Boko, we've been talking all this time and he doesn't even know what I used to do."

"Stop shouting. Tell me your story."

"You'll get bored once you hear it."

"I'll give you a wooden bowl for it."

Qimi agreed and told him the following story:

Qimi used to be a keeper at the barn in the east of the town. When harvest-time came, the straw was transported from the threshing-ground to be stored in the barn. The township's cattle would depend on this fodder in winter. Qimi's work was do all the calculations and prevent fires. Actually, who in the town would want to destroy the barn and risk the lives of their cattle?

Several months before, Qimi had been busy for some time piling up mountains of autumn fodder. Now, once again he had nothing to do. One night, when he felt intolerably bored and was about to fall asleep, he heard someone knock at the door, and he opened up. It was a vagabond who begged for a cup of hot tea. He warmly ushered him into the house, and prepared a pot of beef, and a jar of dense buttered tea, and even dug out a flask of spirits he had buried under the ground of the sheep-pen. The two sat opposite each other with their legs crossed and drank to their satisfaction. Qimi had not enjoyed himself so much for a long time. How many interminable nights he had slept away alone! They consumed over half the spirits and got dead-drunk. At midnight, a man in the town got up to relieve himself, and heard a dog barking. This was so unusual that he looked up at the sky in the east. It was red and his first impression was that it was the light of dawn. Then, he suddenly realized the truth: it was fire. He shouted at the top of his voice. The flames were red and fierce, illuminating the town. Waves of heat hit people as far as two miles away from the heart of the fire. All the townspeople hurried out of their houses in the direction of the barn, but no one came to fight the fire. Several girls stood idly around, examining each other carefully, and found, to their surprise, that their faces had become incredibly rosy and pretty in the heat of the fire; some people skewered meat on a long pole, and stretched it out into the sea of fire, turning it quickly for a minute. When the fragrant aroma wafted out, they drew the pole out and tasted it with satisfaction all the while blowing cold air on the hot meat. Most people just stood around far away and gossiped carelessly and irresponsibly. Everyone knew there was no way to put out the fire, and since to become reincarnated as a

human being was not so easy, who would want to sac-
rifice his precious life? Balls of fire exploded with a deaf-
ening sound as if the earth and mountains had cracked
open. Myriads of small sparks flew hither and thither,
filling the firmament above the town — a spectacular
sight, rarely seen even in a whole century. Some kind,
strong men ran the risk of rushing into the mud-hut beside the blazing piles of grass, and carried out Qimi
and his guest, who, still dead-drunk, didn't even bother to open their eyes when they were thrown into a
ditch. Due to the easy inflammability of the straw, by
the next day hundreds of tons of fodder had fallen vic-
tim to the fierce blaze. High piles of grass were levelled
to the ground. Grey ash covered the black remains of
the straw and thin, upcurling smoke lingered in the air.

Although the fodder for an entire winter had been
completely destroyed, no one wanted to punish Qimi
as they believed that it was not him who had started
the fire and that the only reason he should be condemned was because he had not fulfilled his duty. So,
what the townsmen did was to get the confused vagabond drunk again and then merrily carry him to the
Marqu River near the town, a large group of singing
men and women, young and old following behind.
One man seized his head, the other his feet, and they
swung him in mid-air several times, shouting "One,
two, three, go" in unison, before throwing him into
the river. Water splashed in all directions, then everything returned to its previous tranquillity. The vagabond had not come from this place, and since some
people had seen him coming from the east, they believed the east-flowing water would carry him back to
his hometown.

As cheerfully as ever, the group returned to the town, singing all the way. Now it was time to dispose of Qimi. As responsible and obliging villagers, they couldn't stand by idly. They discussed the matter, helped Qimi to his feet and comforted him with all sorts of kind words. Everyone remained silent on the way to the police station, heads lowered as if in a funeral procession. It was inevitable that they would have to hand Qimi over to the police.

Qimi had escaped from prison seven times. After the fourth time, the police had no alternative but to resort to their magic weapon — the latest wolf-tooth handcuffs which, if a prisoner tried to break free, would automatically become smaller and smaller until the rings of teeth cut through his skin and flesh and pierced deep into the marrow of the bone. Two prisoners had tried them, and Qimi was the third. But Qimi had a pair of wonderful hands unlike anyone else's. His wrist bones and knuckles were unusually soft, and as flexible as rubber, his skin as smooth as oil. Within three minutes he had freed his hands without any difficulty. He waited calmly. Deep into the night, he used the handcuffs as a convenient tool to dig a hole through the wall. Then he crawled out, breathed in deeply the fresh air before dawn and strolled down the road to Luoda Town.

Later Qimi would always say that the reason he had escaped was that there was a sweet dusty smell in the cell which he found quite intolerable.

Jam Waje had heard about the fire, but he was oblivious of its specific details. After listening to Qimi's narration, he did not think it was worth a bowl — he was eager to know why they weren't bothering to arrest him.

"That, I don't know. You'd better ask them."

It was quite true that Qimi had no idea, and just because of this he didn't get the bowl. He was disappointed but that was that.

As he walked out of the teahouse resentfully, he ran
into Melung, who, as expected, invited him to his
house for some delicious mutton.

Qimi was, of course, unlikely to refuse such an invitation.

Melung was a well-known and skilful tailor but
much less well-known as a mechanic. He was secretly
inventing a high-velocity firearm. He had two daughters, the elder beautiful and dissolute, the younger
pretty and imaginative. I'll tell you more about the
Melung family later.

The domestic affairs at Luoda police station were top-
secret. Later, however, someone leaked this informa-
tion: the police in Luoda had no other fetters apart
from handcuffs. They therefore added a new regulation
which was only known to the police force. That was, if
a prisoner succeeded in escaping from prison several
times as Qimi had done, he would not have to serve a
term of imprisonment for his crime.

As evening set in, Qimi walked from Melung's
house to the adjacent toilet, a small pillbox-like struc-
ture with several stone steps leading up to it.

His eyes swept over the whole town: smoke rose
upwards from kitchens and beneath it every house,
which had not been white-washed or painted some other
colour, exposed its original hue — a dusty yellow.

Luoda was a small, dusty yellow town.

Translated by Chen Haiyan

On the Way to Lhasa

IN those days Gyagar Cering, an excellent hunter, had nothing to fear under the sun. His trainer, a native of Kongbo, had spent all his life hunting bears with a sword. He had taught Gyagar Cering this somewhat risky hunting technique. When he was dying, he warned him never to provoke the few brown bears on Mount Gyasong Gumo. He said they were heaven-sent guardians of the mountain and any provocative attempt would bring disaster. Soon after that, he was foolish enough to do what his trainer had warned him not to do — he went up to the mountain to annoy the bears. Gyagar Cering had asked to join the militia of the commune, but the secretary said, because of his unfavourable family background, he had to go up to the mountain to kill harmful animals and bring back their front paws and gall bladders as proof. He had refused at first, but soon he made up his mind to do what the secretary had demanded. He set out on his way, carrying with him provisions for several days, a well-sharpened steel knife tucked under his belt, a half-foot long bamboo stick with sharpened ends, and an especially hard, wicker arm guard bound round with robust ox tendons as strong as steel. He spent two days climbing the mountain from one side and two more days looking for the brown bears which he eventually found by a narrow stream while they were drinking water. There were two of them — the mother bear and her almost-grown son. During the day they ran around, playing; at night they went to sleep in their separate caves. One early dawn, Jaga Tsering tiptoed into the cave of the mother bear and found her curled up like a ball with her back towards the entrance. He edged close enough to scratch her back carefully with the bamboo stick in his left hand, his arm protected by the wicker guard. Feeling comfortable, the bear turned back, thinking he was another bear caressing her with its nuzzle. When she yawned with her mouth wide open, her small eyes still closed, the hunter quickly thrust the hard, sharp bamboo stick into her throat. Feeling a piercing pain, the bear bit hard and the bamboo stick penetrated her upper and lower palates, preventing her from closing her mouth again. Almost at the same moment, the hunter's right hand drove the steel knife into her heart. With a desperate groan straight from the throat and a convulsive shake of the body, the bear breathed her last. Gyagar Cering's shoulder had been clawed by the dying bear and it was so painful that he was in a cold sweat all over. When he entered the other cave, it was already light. The young male bear gazed at the approaching hunter. It must have sniffed the smell of its mother's blood. Gyagar Cering was terrified. He knew that if he turned and ran, the bear would swoop down on him and strike him with its enormous paws. The animal and the man glared at each other in silence, their fury simmering to boiling point. Suddenly, with a violent effort, he threw the knife at the head of the bear and, as the bear raised its paws to fend off the knife, he dashed out of the cave and climbed for his life along

the leather rope he had hung from the cliff beforehand.
The top of the cliff was seven or eight metres high and
just as he was about to make it, the bear grasped the
rope and swung it violently. He swayed back and forth
in mid-air, his head, hurt by the edges of the rocks,
bled and he almost let go of the rope. Finally he got
to the top. He stood there, out of breath, looking
down at the bear. There was a knife-wound at the corner of its mouth that was bubbling with red froth. Staring up at the hunter, the bear roared and then ran off
towards the snow-clad peak in the distance, snarling
up at the sky.

Anyway, with the pair of bear paws, he earned a
certificate of merit and a used semi-automatic rifle for
killing harmful animals. The commune accepted him
into the militia. But he did not tell anybody that the
other bear had escaped.

Maybe because of this foolish deed, he suffered a terrible retribution. A few years later he was jailed for five
years but he managed to escape from prison before he
had served his time. In order to shake off the police,
he turned off the road and onto an old path, used in
ancient times, leading from Kamba in the east to
Lhasa in the west. Along the path a silent boy of
twelve or thirteen years old followed him and he took
him as his travelling companion. Three days later, he
found out that the boy was a mute, but had very sensi-
tive ears. Gyagar Cering called him Po which meant
"boy". Then a young girl by the name of Sang
joined them and the party of three headed for the same
destination — Lhasa.

The winding path unrolled itself through wild grass,

with uninterrupted hills rolling up and down on their right.

"We've passed Mount Tarla," Gyagar Cering said. "It looks as if there is pastureland ahead."

"In fact, we can now turn onto the road and ask for a lift there," Sang said. "They can't capture you halfway along the road."

"I have a better idea." Gyagar Cering was not tall but strongly-built, with short hair and slanting eyes. He stripped himself to the waist and Po did the same.

"They are not likely to run into us face to face on this road," Sang added.

"A fat lot you know!" Gyagar Cering raised his voice. "You silly fool."

Po's big bright eyes flashed. He was able to keep pace with the adults and concentrate on their conversation at the same time.

"You said I'm a fool." Sang could not dismiss the insult from her mind, her full attractive breasts heaving up and down. She was carrying a light pack and, as the brass cooker had come loose, she took it off the pack and held it in her hand, her face tight with anger.

"Don't think I'm safe here. I've seen not a few prisoners recaptured." He looked back and asked: "Haven't you noticed anything suspicious since we teamed up?"

"No."

"You're no more than a brainless female ass with big breasts."

"Bang!" Sang hit him on the back with her brass cooker and, before he had recovered balance, swung it round and hit his belly hard. He knelt on the ground, holding his belly with his hands, groaning.

Seeing there was no one else, not even a hare around, Sang squatted down next to Gyagar Cering and said, caressing his face with her hand, "Don't you ever swear at me again!"

"What a pernicious woman you are! You've beaten the shit out of me." He stood up and, holding his stomach with both hands, walked towards the grass where the land was lower.

Up in the high blue sky there was only one eagle gliding around.

The three of them sat on the ground for a rest, surrounded by the quiet and desolate grassland. As there was no wood to make a fire, they could not make tea. That day when Gyagar Cering and Po passed Sang's village, even she herself did not know why she had fallen in love with that fellow who had several prominent scars around his waist. When he came that evening to fumble at the bolt of her gate, being rather clumsy, he made a clanking noise. Her brother, with his hunting gun in his hand, caught him. When he learned that this tramp was also a huntsman, he entertained him with wine and warned him never to touch his sister again. But as soon as he was drunk and had fallen fast asleep, Gyagar Cering took Sang by the hand and ran off....

For a few moments, Po's sharp eyes stared at a point in the distance and when Sang turned her head and looked in the same direction, she said:

"There's a man on top of the hill."

"How many?" Gyagar Cering asked, without looking up.

"One."

"That's him."

"That's who?" Sang asked.

"I don't know."

"What's he up to?"

"What's he up to? You go and ask him your-self."

"He can't be a policeman, can he?" Sang asked again.

Po shook his head.

"A policeman," Sang giggled.

"He is far away from here, so far off that he can't even hear a whistle." Sang turned and took another look, saying in a low voice, "I hope it's not my brother coming after us."

In the distance, on top of the highest of the rolling hills, there stood a figure, looking like a tiny black sil-houette.

Gyagar Cering was aware that the man had been fol-lowing them for the past two days and on the third day, he was sure to appear in front of him. This was an old-fashioned custom of the Kamba people who lived on the Lancang River and in the eastern areas.

With his extreme sensitivity he smelled a sweetness in the air which had been around for quite some time. He disliked the smell because there was something ominous about it.

A gust of cold wind brushed across the clean wild grassland without stirring up any dust. It blew with a rustle of grass and a coolness of air towards the horizon.

Towards evening they came to a livestock farm where there were four tents constructed of black cow hide. Several sheep dogs as big as calves kept barking at them. The dogs were tethered to a wooden stake by one of the tents and as they jumped, they dragged the stake loose and charged at them in a frenzy of violence. Two pigtailed young girls rushed out from the tent and held the dogs tight by the neck with their arms.

Having learned that the host of one of the tents had a collection of first-rate knives, Gyagar Cering went to see him. He took off two beads from his turquoise necklace hoping to trade them for a knife. The small, scrawny host held the two beads in his hand, scrutinizing them by the fire. He thought for a moment and then, shaking his head, gave them back to him. Gyagar Cering took off another one and threw it to him. He seemed to be satisfied and put them in his pocket. He went to a corner of the tent and took out seven or eight long knives from a leather bag and, throwing them next to the fire, told him to choose whichever he pleased. When he saw the knives he knew in an instant that the host had not let him down. Except for one long British style-bayonet, sheathed in leather, they were all precious ones of exquisite workmanship, well-greased and well-preserved. Turning them over for a long while, he set his eyes on a shorter one which looked old and rough. The sheath was made of two thick bamboo clappers tied together with cow tendon and steel wires, the handle wrapped round with goat leather. When he unsheathed the knife he was dazzled by a cold bluish light. Flicking it with his fingers, he was satisfied with the sound it produced. After putting the edge of the knife against his front teeth and scratching them lightly, he said, knife in hand, "I'll take this one."

"Good for you! You've taken the best of the bunch."

"Haha! Are you going to back out?"

"No. Nothing of the sort," the herdsman said. "Since you know about knives, take it."

To celebrate the successful deal, the herdsman fetched a bottle of wine and uncorked it with his teeth. He placed the bottle in the middle of a table made of earth. The two men sat opposite each other. The host said his daughter was getting married and she needed a couple of turquoises for ornamentation. While telling him the story about his daughter, he urged Gyagar Cering to drink.

"Are you a huntsman?"

Gyagar Cering nodded.

"I thought you were, with the scars on your chest, the way you picked out the knife. Are you taking any game with you since you are going to Lhasa?"

"I am going to settle in Lhasa if I can find a job there."

"That's right. There isn't much left to hunt in the mountains these days. Everyone's heading for Lhasa. Are you going there for the first time?"

"Yes."

"Since you are already very close to Lhasa, what do you want a knife for? There is not much to hunt around here."

Gyagar Cering just went on drinking. A moment later, he said, "I am escaping from prison."

The host handed over the bottle to him, scratching his forehead with his fingers. Gyagar Cering took a few more swigs.

"No wonder your face looks as white as a ghost.

Are they still after you?''

"I expect so.''

"I can lend you a couple of horses and, when you get to Lhasa, you can leave them with my relative there.''

"No, thanks,'' he mumbled, wiping his mouth with the back of his hand. "I have no idea who is following me.''

The host took a few mouthfuls of wine, his eyes fixed on Jaga Tsering.

"Let me tell you something. The chief of the work team was loud and opinionated. I didn't like the manner in which he spoke and I hit him. In those days I did not believe what he said. I asked him what mistakes Chairman Mao had made. He was God, I said. I wanted to testify right there and then. As I was a militia man, I could shoot very well. I placed the *Quotations of Chairman Mao* at the foot of a tree at the end of the village and nobody dared to stop me because I had a gun in my hand. All the villagers had gathered around. Standing at a hundred feet from the book, I took aim. With luck I hit the book and the bullet went right through. I was really an excellent shot. Well, when they sentenced me to five years in prison I had nothing to say. If he was really God, you could not have hit it, but I did. Of course, I did not complain.''

The herdsman let out a whistle, "You want to ward off bullets with a knife?''

"He'll get to me ahead of the police.'' So saying, he stood up and went out of the tent without looking back.

"Who are you talking about?'' the host asked

from inside the tent.

"A personal enemy."

Outside the tent, the effect of the wine wore off. There was a fire flaring in the distance where Sang was waiting for him. Po was curled up on the ground next to the fire, wrapped in a thin blanket. There was a nip in the night air and the sky was dotted with stars. The dim outline of the rolling hills was just visible, the river on the other side glimmering with faint white light. It was quiet on the farm.

Gyagar Cering sat by the fire which burned cowdung. He drank the tea but not the food Sang had prepared for him. He had drunk too much wine and his temples throbbed visibly.

Sang spotted the knife tucked under his belt. Moving over to him, she slowly pulled out the knife from the sheath, poked the fire with it, a cloud of sparks going up instantly. She thrust the knife at his feet.

"I don't like this. You are outnumbered and your knife is no match for their guns," she said in a resentful tone.

"Sang, please listen to me," he said, running his fingers through his hair. "As it is not my fault, nothing will happen to us."

"I don't believe you! I don't believe you!"

"Don't shout and wake Po up."

"When I first met you, you were not like this. You sang songs, you had a sense of humour and you were as happy as an immortal. I was really happy then."

"Sang!"

"You'd better fly away alone like an eagle and I won't clip your wings at all. I've got my own feet and I can walk by myself."

Gyagar Cering swung his fist and knocked her to the ground.

Late at night, the dogs outside the tents barked a couple of times and then once again the grassland was engulfed in deep silence.

In the darkness they whispered to each other.

"I trust you," Sang said tenderly.

"My little nightingale."

"Ah! My darling!" Sang grasped his hair and shook his head vigorously. Stretching out her neck, she banged her forehead against his.

When Gyagar Cering woke up at midnight, he felt that something was wrong. Somewhere in the darkness, somebody must have been lying in wait. The night was so dark that he felt restless. He thought that the man — the strange enemy — must have followed him to revenge his father.

Two decades ago, Gyagar Cering's father had killed Gomchen, the chief of a gang of horse thieves, nicknamed "Long Face". His father had been an actor in a Tibetan drama troupe in Hatang district, when he was young, and later he teamed up with Gomchen, roaming about in the Kamba area. Gyagar Cering had never been able to make out why his father had got into a fight with the big bandit Gangqin, nor had his mother ever told him about it. One night, his father returned, his clothes smeared with blood. He told his wife, gasping, that he had to go into hiding somewhere and then he went away, leaving his wife and son on their own. He went to India, never to be heard of again. Jaga Tsering remembered that his father used to sing as he drank and one of the songs he enjoyed singing went like this: "Although this fiddle is full of music, you cannot get the tunes right. If you are not ready to play when the dance starts up in time with the song, don't blame me if I skin you alive and use your skin for a wooden ladle." After his father escaped, his mother went with him to a remote village and settled there. Whenever he thought of his father, he felt like singing that song but hardly had he got the first line out when his mother stopped his mouth with her hand for fear the song would betray who they were and their enemy would learn their whereabouts. Later, when he was herding the sheep on the hills one day, he wanted to sing it, but he could not recollect the words or the tune.

Towards evening, a wind blew up, sweeping across the length and breadth of the grassland. The sky was overcast with black clouds, thunder rumbling on the horizon. It was getting cold. Gyagar Cering and Po came to a village at the head of which they found a small tavern and they walked in cheerfully.

The light in the tavern was faint. A few flies buzzed around the pillar in the middle of the room. Two or three farmhands were drinking at a table. Gyagar Cering and Po found a table at a corner. Jaga Tsering was in a very good mood because it was a long time since he had been to a tavern. When he looked through the door in the partition wall, he saw a woman in the inner room pouring wine from a big barrel into a pot. She began to sing with a heavy Chamdo accent, oblivious to the presence of the others, "Without being invited, I've come to see the hostess and before she touches her lip to the cup I'll be dead drunk.'' All the farmhands looked askance at the unrestrained vagrant, but none of them dared stand up and stop her. The hostess, her face glowing with the radiance of youth, floated out with the wine pot in her hands. She was very attractive, with a pair of dimples dancing on her cheeks. In exchanging casual remarks she revealed that she was from Kamba too and was married in this area seven or eight years ago.

After they had taken a few cups of wine, Po nudged Gyagar Cering with his elbow and pointed towards the door, meaning that it was going to rain and Sang had not returned.

"She can find us here.'' Turning to the woman, he asked: "Sister, can we stay here for this one night?''

"Of course. I can put you two up all right.''

"And we've got Sang with us too.''

"A girl?''

"Yes.''

"All right.'' She went to the inner room.

"Did you hear? She said 'All right.''' He turned to Po.

Po poked himself in the belly with his fingers.

"Sister, have you got anything to eat?''

"We serve wine only,'' she answered from the inner room.

"My brother says he is so hungry that he is going to eat his own fist.''

"Will pancakes do?''

"Yes!'' he answered in a loud voice.

The few farmhands watched this devil-may-care traveller with indignation in their eyes. As he drank, Gyagar Cering tilted his head backward, looking at the ceiling. After several cupfuls, when he pulled the pot over and wanted to refill his cup, Po grabbed the cup from his hand, gesticulating with his open hand over his own face.

"Are you saying I'm drunk, my face as red as a piece of red cloth?" He snatched his cup back, pushed Po aside and refilled it. "Don't interfere with me, you secretive little devil! I won't have it. I simply can't bear to look at you. Sang and you and I are going to live together, but not the way we have been, like donkeys."

The woman came out with a plateful of deep-fried cakes and a bowlful of beef, stir-fried with potato chips.

"I've got some spirits, do you want it?" she asked.

"Thanks." Gyagar Cering held her soft hand and pressed it against his forehead.

Suddenly the sky, heavily overcast with black clouds, released a stormy downpour — first sparse drops of rain drumming the ground, then a noisy splash of falling water. Some passers-by stepped in to keep away from the rain, making excited comments under the awning.

A dazzling flash of lightning lit up the sky and almost at the same moment a figure flashed into the tavern. "Kahh, Kahh ..." There was a clap of thunder, as if the sky were exploding and the earth splitting. The shriek of a woman was heard in the distance. The lamps in the tavern flickered a few times.

Still gripped by the aftermath of the thunder, the customers caught sight of a young Kamba fellow sitting at a far corner, his back towards the door, a cup placed in front of him. His face was emaciated but formidably resolute. His clothes were dripping with water and a trickle was flowing from his wide-rimmed hat down to his shoulders. His white shirt clung to his chest prominently revealing two hard lumps of muscle. A strand of a red fringe hung from one side of his forehead and his eyes under long lashes shed a cold sombre light.

"Sister, wine, please," he ordered in a controlled voice, but it was clearly heard against the thunders rumbling outside.

"Look! You are flooding tavern with the water you've brought in." The woman had to shout to drown the splashing sounds of the rain. She picked up the corner of her apron to wipe off the water from his face, but he stopped her. He patted her cheek with his fingers and then pointed at the empty cup on the table.

Gyagar Cering was awakened by the clap of thunder. He knew by the terrified look in Po's eyes that the man had come at last. Resting his chin in both hands, he grinned oddly at Po. By now he had become aware of the fact that Sang had been out begging for food for quite a while and she had not yet come back. He knew that she would be able to find him in the tavern but he did not wish her to return at this moment.

"Sister, wine, please," he ordered, looking at Po.

"Aiya, you are turning me around like a spindle. Why don't you sit at the same table and have fun together since you are all from Kamba? Come on."

"There is no hurry, sister," Gyagar Cering said in composure. "We will have fun together."

Po stood up, walked over to Gyagar Cering and sat next to him. The stranger, holding his cup in his hand, came up from behind Jaga Tsering and took the seat opposite that Po had left empty. His green canvas shoes with rubber soles were completely worn out, his toes, soaked white by the rain, sticking out. Around his waist there was a leather bag which looked like a cartridge belt. People in the eastern areas liked to wear these for carrying bank notes and precious tools. There was a hunting knife in a silver sheath, tucked in at his waist. The smell must have come from him, Gyagar Cering thought, but when he sat across from him, the odour disappeared.

The rain had settled down to a monotonous, steady beat, its violence abating. The incessant rain trickled down from the eaves with an irritating sound, making one feel sleepy and depressed. Having come to the end of their patience, some of the customers dashed out into the rain with their heads wrapped in their arms.

"What delightful rain!" taking a swig of wine, the stranger remarked softly, his eyes looking out of the window.

"And so is the wine — the first round," Gyagar Cering said, feeling a current of heat sweeping from across the table. It was the heat vaporizing through the stranger's wet clothes.

"I haven't been in a tavern for a long time."

"Take care not to get drunk."

Po cocked his head against Gyagar Cering's chest and the latter lovingly put his arm round Po's scrawny shoulder.

"Your brother?" the stranger asked.

"Everybody says he is. Any resemblance?"

"The mouth and the head."

"You've got a good eye."

Po looked at the stranger with a touch of loneliness

in his eyes.

"Sang often hits him on the backside. She hit him with her brass cooker last night," Gyagar Cering added.

"The locals here are too bad," the stranger said, his head hanging low. "With just two ladlefuls of *tsamba* they'll try to drag her into their houses."

"She is not a kitten. They'll get a taste of her medicine."

"Right." The stranger smiled. "She knows how to protect herself. The local men ... sh — Is she your woman?" He looked towards the door, his eyes brightening up.

"Hey! You men must be hungry," Sang's voice rang out. She strode in with a leather bag filled with food, her clothes dripping wet. She spotted the stranger in surprise, and sat down next to him. Wiping off the water from her face and lifting the bag onto the table, she turned to him and asked: "How are you, brother?"

The stranger raised his eyebrows and looked warmly at her.

"I'm as soaked as you are," Sang said. "Are you following us?"

"Heading in a different direction."

"I thought you were my brother following us." Turning to Jaga Tsering, she asked, "Don't you think he looks like my brother?"

"In a way."

"He has the same habits." Her eyebrows went up, imitating the stranger. "We four can pair up to play cards. I'm sure you will win."

Gyagar Cering noticed that the brass buttons on her

red shirt had been ripped off, the front of her shirt torn open, breasts visible scratched and smeared with blood.

"Is your cooker twisted from hitting?" Gyagar Cering teased her.

"The cooker?" She shook the pack on her back, the cooker jangling there. "I didn't use it. I was afraid their heads were not strong enough."

She smiled with pride. She turned and asked the stranger, "What's your name?"

"Tradu."*

Gyagar Cering did not seem to hear. When Sang looked at him, he was putting his ring finger into his cup, trying to pick a fly out of it.

There was a moment's silence.

"I hear, a couple of days ago, they were searching for a prison escapee at the checkpoint," Tradu said.

"Do you mean on the road?"

"They've got your photo, checking it against every passer-by."

"I see."

"They seemed to know you were taking this road."

"What about you? You don't wish me to be taken back, do you?"

"Are you a policeman?" Sang edged over and asked.

"No, he isn't," Gyagar Cering said.

"You shouldn't have escaped," Tradu said.

"Why not?" Sang was puzzled. "He's a man, not a sheep in the fold. He's told everything. Sentenced to five years in prison just because he hit the chief of the work team?"

---

*In Tibetan this means conquering personal enemies.

"More. There is more to it — what happened earlier."

Sang looked at Gyagar Cering who, in turn, looked at Tradu with hatred in his eyes. After a moment, he said at a controlled pace, "She is not supposed to know any more. It's all behind us already. Neither of us has experienced it personally, have we?"

"That's right," Tradu said.

The hostess brought beef, wine, tea and a small plate with a little chilli sauce on it.

"Can I stay here for one night?" Tradu asked.

"Fortunately my husband is not at home. He's a coward," the woman said. "He's gone to build the county power station with the construction team. He comes back for a visit once every two weeks. I am alone at the moment."

Po did not understand why the woman with a flush on her face had to chatter away like this.

"Of course you can." She went into the inner room.

When she was half way through the meal, Sang turned and asked Tradu, "Did he cause any trouble to you in the past?"

"Sang!" Gyagar Cering stopped her. "This is our first meeting today."

"You are cheating me."

"He's telling the truth." Tradu was busy eating. "You should not know too much of what happened in the past."

Sang watched the stranger who bent over the table and Po, sitting next to Gyagar Cering, turned his eyes to the window where outside night had fallen.

There was silence except for the dull sound of chewing food and the patter of the rain outside.

The woman brought a few woollen mattresses and a worn-out woollen quilt and they each found a place in the corner. Heavy-hearted, they kept quiet throughout the night. Tradu had obviously rejected the woman's offer, falling into his dreamland and snoring lightly.

Gyagar Cering seemed perplexed — was this the son of that Gomchen? He was not as strongly built as he, thought he would be. When was he going to make a move? Oh, it was all up to him, now.

Before it was light, he had a terrifying dream: a pair of hands thrust out from a crack in the ground and a voice shouted: "Don't kill, you stupid fool!" The hands looked like his father's one minute and Tradu's the next. When he pinched them they hurt and they turned out to be his own. When he took a closer look at them, they grew big and rough and covered with thick hair.

It was a crescent-shaped mountain pass, the top of which was strewn with huge round boulders and a little way below it were the ruins of a temple surrounded by a few dead trees. A narrow winding road zigzagged at the foot of the mountain and disappeared behind a massive rock. From time to time, clouds of dust, stirred by passing trucks, rolled along the road. It was about three or four hours' walk from the pass to the road.

It was a golden dusk. As the sun set dark shadows crept up from below.

Tradu was lying on his back on a rock, his hat over his eyes. This long-time young vagrant set a small tape-recorder by his ear as he often did. Apart from the eastern folk songs familiar to Gyagar Cering and Sang, he enjoyed listening to songs by a certain woman singer. Her unaccompanied voice was husky but very emotional. Tradu told Sang the singer was his mistress. As the batteries were running out, the voice fluctuated and the melody sounded flat. Tradu switched it off.

With his hat over his face, he seemed to have fallen asleep. After a moment, he said, "They've found you, the police."

Gyagar Cering was putting up a stove. He dropped the rocks and with composure straightened up to look towards the north.

"Not possible," he said.

"This afternoon the sun was shining on my face and I felt hot," Tradu said. "When I turned my face I saw them. They were not behind us, but on the mountain in front. I saw a flash, the kind of flash reflected from a mirror."

"Field-glasses."

"However, they won't be able to get here until lunch time tomorrow at the soonest. They are blocked by the river and there is no ferry across."

Shrugging his shoulder with a "hmm", Gyagar Cering went on with his business. Po came, holding Sang's arm. She had sprained her ankle and she said she would have a hard time walking downhill.

"When I sat there rubbing my ankle, I seemed to notice a figure on the hillside over there. When I walked towards it, it was no longer there," Sang recalled.

Tradu moistened his parched lips with his tongue and scratched the areas under his eyes with his small finger, with a tinge of suspicion on his face.

Gyagar Cering was on the verge of throwing the twig in his hand at Tradu, but he desperately contained his rage.

"Maybe, I didn't see clearly because my eyes were blurred with sweat," Sang said. Seeing there was not much firewood left, she took Gyagar Cering's hunting knife and limped around the ruins to cut some. Po went with her.

"Tell him to come out," Gyagar Cering said mockingly. "We've got hot tea here."

"Who?"

"Your friend."

"My friend?" Tradu was puzzled but soon realized what he meant. "You're very suspicious."

"Sang saw him."

"But she said her eyes were blurred. You heard that, didn't you?"

"I don't care a damn." Jutting out his chin and squinting his eyes, he flashed a contemptuous smile at Tradu.

"I just don't want Sang to see him. Otherwise I don't care a damn."

"She's a nice girl and she won't poke her nose into our affairs. It's something between us men, isn't it?"

"That's why I don't care."

Sang and Po returned, carrying a large bundle of dry firewood. She knelt in front of the stove, feeding the fire. She knew very well what had been said between these two indifferent-looking men. As she had promised, she was not going to ask any more questions. The fire flared up quickly, illuminating the night with red leaping flames. With the heat glowing on their faces, they were possessed by a sense of languor.

Gyagar Cering sat cross-legged. He took out the pack of worn-out playing cards, shuffling them skilfully.

"There're four of us, the right number for a game."

"What game?" Tradu asked.

"I'll show you. It's simple."

"I think I can learn it." Tradu seemed to be interested. He held his cards in his hand, spreading them out into a fan. But the first card he dealt was wrong.

The smell was like blood in the mouth, something unfamiliar. He tucked the cards he had won under his leg. He reflected with indignation: I have had it, though I have not committed murder. I am forced into a situation like this. Up until then he was still in the dark about who had harboured a grudge against him.

"Kill it!" He shouted, throwing a card down.

"Ha, ha!" Proudly, Sang showed one of her cards. She then bent over to look at Tradu's cards. "Ah! You've won."

"Have I?" he still did not know how to play the game.

Gyagar Cering thrust his last card right under Tradu's nose and in front of Sang's eyes.

"Aiyo!" Sang put out her tongue at Tradu, saying, "He's won. He's got more points."

"Has he?"

"This is the Senior Devil," Sang explained to Tradu. "Who'll take the punishment?"

. Po covered his mouth with his hands.

"Is it you? All right, I'll take it for you. I enjoy taking punishments." Sang turned her face towards

Gyagar Cering who stepped a few paces backward and took out a couple of dry beans from his pocket.

"How are you going to take it?" Tradu did not know what was going to happen.

"He's going to shoot the beans into my mouth," Sang said. "I like that."

She opened her mouth wide, with her eyes closed, her long lashes fluttering restlessly. Gyagar Cering flicked one of the beans with his thumb and the bean flew right into her mouth, probably down her throat.

"Ah!" She opened her eyes wide and, with a strenuous effort, gulped the bean down and then burst into laughter. "Good Heavens! You are killing me."

Sang sprang over to him, and held his neck in her arms. They rolled over and over on the ground, laughing. Stealing a glance at Tradu, Po was surprised to find him watching them with a sweet smile dancing at the corners of his mouth.

It was getting dark and soon they all lay with their clothes on around the fire, except for Gyagar Cering. He lifted Sang's head and put it on his leg, watching her face in silence. In silence, she now watched his eyes, now the stars in the sky. They watched each other like that for a long while.

"Your hair is growing long," Sang said in a soft voice, feeling his hair with her hand.

"It grows very slow."

"Let it grow very long. I've prepared a pair of tassels for you." She took out a pair of silk red ones.

"Take good care of them for me."

"Yes. I'll put them on for you in due course."

Sang realized that it was almost impossible for her to

get to know about things that concerned men, much less for her to change them.

"I am really sleepy." She slowly closed her eyes with a miserable smile on her face. After a long pause her breathing settled down to an even, steady rhythm. Carefully lifting her head off his legs, he stood up, heaving a deep sigh. "There is nothing else I need to worry about now," he said to himself.

A crescent moon rose from behind the mountain. Putting some dry firewood into the fire, he then walked towards the darkness. He shivered with the chill of the night. He came to a slope behind the temple ruins where stood a large round rock twice his height, leaning over as if about to fall over at any moment. He stood against the rock, motionless, refreshing himself in the cold air. The mountains far and near remained as dim outlines. Not far off a few sparks flashed, enhancing the tenderness of the night. He was reminded of an old saying popular in his hometown: Seize the night and run with your sweetheart.

The sweetish smell was in the air again and, suddenly, Gyagar Cering was seized by terror.

He came, closer with each step, and stopped two paces below Jaga Tsering. He stood legs apart, his hat pulled down low over his forehead and his hand on his knife, exactly the way he had appeared in front of him the first time.

"Are you going to tell me a long story?" Gyagar Cering asked.

Tradu stood motionless, like a rock, the night air getting thicker and heavier. Gyagar Cering could hardly believe his ears when in a deliberate and grave manner, the story was related to him.

Finally the strong-willed woman released the two "eagles" she had brought up through those years of hardship. The two brothers had spent three years in search of their foe, but they had returned empty-handed. Their mother set out again, telling them that if they failed to find their enemy they should never come back to her. This thought tormented them. But though they did not find the enemy, they each found a girl. The older brother said he was not going to lead a wanderer's life any more and his girl taught him how to operate a tractor. The younger brother begged him over and over again, but he wouldn't change his mind. He insisted on going to his girl, Rinzin Wangmo. The younger brother begged him on his knees not to leave him, but he said, "That's enough! Even if I found him I wouldn't stab him. Besides, I don't know him at all." Unable to bear listening to him any longer, the younger brother jumped up and knocked him down to the ground. After that the brothers separated, each going off his own way, one to his girlfriend, the other to search for his father's enemy....

"Damn the younger brother." Gyagar Cering closed his eyes, his hand on the knife.

"In less than a month after we parted," Tradu said, "I ran into you here."

"You pernicious wolf," Gyagar Cering spat at the ground.

Through the misty light of the crescent moon, Gyagar Cering saw Tradu pulling out his knife and pointing it at him, his face contorted. All this happened as quickly as lightning and Gyagar Cering stood dumb-founded. With a look of fear and desperation in his eyes, Tradu arched his back like a cat ready to fight a snake, his throat uttering a strange noise, "Stand still! Don't move!"

When Gyagar Cering pulled out his knife, Tradu, screaming, started charging at him. Just as he raised his knife to defend himself, he was suddenly swept to the ground by an enormous black thing from above, his knife spinning out of his hand. He felt a splitting pain in his shoulder. Rolling on the ground, he dodged out of Tradu's way. Damn it, there was another one lying in wait behind me, after all. He knew he was severely wounded. Suddenly, in the darkness, he ran into Tradu's knife. He held the steel of the knife tight and its edge cut deep into his palm. He raised his knife and swung it around. The tip of the knife must have penetrated very deep, for a gush of hot sticky blood oozed onto his hand and down to his elbow. He saw clearly Tradu's ear dangling against his neck.

Po jumped up, rubbing his eyes with the back of his hand. He had smelled something burning — the corner of his jacket with which he had covered himself had caught fire. He stamped on the jacket frantically until the fire was put out. When he looked around, he found the two men missing. Panic-stricken, he went looking hither and thither in the dark. Suddenly he broke into a run like a wild animal, screaming with unintelligible sounds.

Gyagar Cering now looked like a man of blood, his jacket in shreds, a few pieces of flesh coming loose from his bones. The finger joints of the hand which had held the edge of the knife had become stiff, for the knife had cut into the marrow. It was not possible to open his hand again. Breathing heavily, he could not stand straight because a large portion of his bowels had flowed out from the right-hand side of his belly.

It was dead quiet. The moon was obscured by a moving cloud. In the far distance rolled the rumbling of trucks on their way to Lhasa. Soon the trucks could be heard no more.

On a terrace not far from Gyagar Cering there loomed an enormous vaguely-shaped black thing. Ever since the male bear had been injured by the hunter, it had never forgotten his smell. For ten years, it had been searching for him with a strong and perpetual sense of vengeance. Finally it had revenged itself. Its body, now stiff, lay on the hill like a black tomb.

"Hey, my friend!" Gyagar Cering called in his husky voice.

"I'm dying." The voice came from an invisible place nearby. In a moment, the same voice was heard again, "I never expected it to come down on me."

"As a matter of fact, the bear did not come for you, he came for me." While he spoke his mouth bubbled with blood, smelling of a sweetish smell.

"My friend," he called again. "You're not dying, because you have not finished your story yet."

He was groaning in the darkness:

"It's the end for me. Rinzin Wangmo is still waiting for me, but I cannot move any more."

Knowing that Tradu was not far from him, Gyagar Cering slowly moved forward, groping about on the ground. Suddenly he thought of the song his father had been fond of singing. He was sure he could sing it now. Making one last effort and swallowing a mouthful of blood, he managed to turn over and lie on his back. Looking up at the high and desolate sky, he began to sing crescendo in a melancholy, sonorous voice:

"Ai ... although this fiddle is full of music...."

Tradu joined him in a soft weak voice:

"Hai ... Ai...."

"You can't get the tunes right."

"Hai ... Ai...."

"If you're not ready to play when the dance starts up in time with the song,"

"Hai ... Ai...."

"Don't blame me if I skin you alive and use your skin for a wooden ladle."

"Hai ... Ai...." The accompaniment stopped short. Then there was a long moment of silence until the moon came out of the clouds again....

Po headed towards where the song came from. Against the moonlight, he saw a scene which he would never be able to forget for the rest of his life: Tradu was dead — half of his face, one ear left, was in shreds, his chest ripped open with a few ribs laid bare. Gyagar Cering was lying head to head with him, his right hand still holding the knife.

"Ah, ah!" Po knelt down by Gyagar Cering who still had his eyes open, but unable to move, his chest heaving up and down. Looking at Po out of the corner of his eyes, he spoke in a barely audible voice, "It's better to remain mute."

That afternoon, the three policemen who had been following him arrived on the scene. They saw the enormous dead bear lying on the slope. The splashes of blood on the ground had congealed. Strewn in the blood were shreds of cloth, strands of hair and a broken tape recorder. Overhead in the sky a large flock of eagles were gliding around. Shocked, they climbed onto a large rock by the pass, looking downhill through their field-glasses.

Two figures were moving slowly downward, dragging two corpses behind them. The sloping path was precipitous and, with every step they took, loose rocks crashed down to the foot of the mountain.

The crash of the rolling rocks echoed back and forth throughout the valley.

Translated by Liu Shicong

The Silent Sage

AS the last sounds of the closing door gradually receded, the mansion settled back into eerie silence. The toothless old gate-keeper anxiously cast an eye over the grounds, though the chance of burglars intruding was slim: the place was so forbidding that even dogs slunk by with their tails between their legs, despite there being a hole in the wall that seemed tailor-made for them.

In the clean, neatly paved courtyard, apple trees swayed gently in the breeze, their slowly-ripening fruit swelling on the branches like young girls' breasts. The white-washed walls of the mansion reflected the sunlight and dazzled prying eyes, which were discouraged further by its somber, large black windows. A pair of rusty copper knockers hung from the half-open gate.

Suddenly the old man paused with a sense of foreboding. Every morning at exactly the same time the telephone would ring in the front left room on the second floor, its piercing tone splitting the air and disturbing the tranquil atmosphere of the courtyard.

Now he waited expectantly, looking up from time to time at the window. He braced himself, unable to settle until the sound had come and gone.

The young master of the house had left a few minutes earlier. The servant had opened the gate and the young man had emerged wearing a silver helmet and pushing a bright red motorcycle. Outside the gate he had joined a similarly-clad, mean-looking group who were sitting on their machines and waiting for him in silence.

The respectful "Sir" murmured by the servant to his master was lost in the wind as the bikes roared away like stampeding horses, leaving him covered in a cloud of dust.

The young man was basically a nice fellow. He was a journalist who, more than anything else, enjoyed physical exercise.

But not a single sound ever emerged from inside the walls of the house — not even from a TV or radio, despite the presence of an aerial on the roof. The old man hadn't the slightest idea what went on in there or how his master lived: his job was simply to open and close the gate, which he did at frequent intervals, and to cultivate the garden and ensure the courtyard was kept immaculate. The high points in his life were when the master returned from a consultative congress press conference in a limousine. The car would honk impatiently at the gate and old Toothless would scurry out of his little mud shack and heave open the iron gates. The master would be seated in the back and hidden behind dark tinted windows; no one could see what he looked like.

Half an hour went by and the phone still didn't ring.

The gate-keeper pushed open the door of his shack and peered out. An old beggar sat crouched in the corner by the gate. Next to him, a melancholy-looking goat, smelling to high heaven, squatted on its haunches.

"Do you know that you've been sitting there for twenty years?" asked the gate-keeper. It was the first time he had ever addressed the old crock, who started and opened one eye. "Yet you've never even been given a piece of bread or a cup of tea," he continued, "it's a wonder you haven't starved."

"I'm a sage," said the miserable creature, his first utterance sounding thick and hoarse.

"Be careful what you say, or I'll call the police," threatened the gate-keeper.

The old man narrowed his eyes until they were barely more than a slit.

"You've been waiting for a phone call, haven't you?"

The porter was flabbergasted. Maybe he really was a sage after all.

The senile old goat let out a querulous bleat.

"You should shoo it away," advised the servant.

"I can't. It keeps following me around. It knows everything."

The gate-keeper warned him that if he wasn't careful he would get run over by the master's car. But the old sage wasn't listening. He began scratching at lice beneath his shaggy blanket, and the servant regretted having spoken. "I shouldn't have bothered," he said. "After all, I've managed to ignore you for twenty years. This is a bad sign."

"Who is the call for?" inquired the old sage.

"Not me. It's for the master's sister — a spinster."

"And who calls?" persisted the sage with growing curiosity.

"I can't tell you," said the servant, shaking his head.

"You should have told me that earlier," answered the sage irritably.

The gate-keeper stared at him and, stressing every syllable, said, "You are bad news."

The sage looked back in alarm. Then, abruptly, he fell silent.

The gate-keeper was right. That afternoon the young master was brought home on a stretcher. Bullets had ripped through his head so violently that he was hardly recognizable. Preliminary investigations by the police indicated that he had been involved in some shady dealings. Apparently he had agreed to buy twenty-thousand yuan worth of gold from a smuggler he'd met in a mountain valley. Intending to take the loot without paying for it, he'd taken along with him a martial arts specialist. But the dealer had the same intention and when the young master and his companion sprang on him, the dealer pulled out a pistol and shot the two of them, though his companion managed to escape by feigning death.

The courtyard suddenly became alive with activity as policemen traipsed back and forth trying to find out what had happened. They even took the gate-keeper aside for in-depth questioning.

Finally they left, and only the old sage remained, still sitting by the gate.

"The young master's dead," said the gate-keeper, eyeing him coldly. "You really are a bad omen."

The sage lowered his head, and didn't reply.

The goat stretched out its neck and bleated anxiously.

The courtyard gradually settled back into its usual state of austere tranquillity; not a sound could be heard, but the hair rose on the back of the servant's neck and for a moment he was afraid to go back in, preferring even to have the old crock with him. Suddenly he noticed that the goat's eyes seemed to have become human and were staring into his own. Their shape, their expression, the blinking lids and rolling eyeballs seemed to contain vital thoughts and profound wisdom. They seemed to be sadly pleading with him. "What's the matter with the goat?" cried the servant, shrinking back in fear. He turned and ran into his shack, reappearing moments later with a large club with which he intended to drive the wretched animal away.

"When I was twelve years old," said the sage, fixing his eyes on the club, "I borrowed someone's horse to ride down to the river where I played. When I got back my brother thrashed me so hard I had to stay in bed for three days. Strangely enough, he died a few days later, because it turned out that I was the reincarnation of the Living Buddha. Then, a few years ago, I ran into this goat, which I recognized immediately to be my brother reincarnated. His punishment for beating me — the reincarnation of Living Buddha — had been to be transformed into an animal."

The gate-keeper remembered having heard once before of a case involving the reincarnation of the Living Buddha and wondered whether the two could be related. Many years before, when the house had been owned by a colonel, the servant's own father had been gate-keeper. One day he had emerged to find a beggar woman, with two small children in her arms, occupying exactly the same spot as the sage. A generous man, he had given the woman some left-over food, but even after she had eaten the woman refused to leave, saying that her baby would kick up too much of a fuss. Sure enough, when she stood up the baby began screaming and kicking like a thing possessed. While this was going on a group of officials on horseback arrived on the scene. They said they had come from the west in search of a boy said to be the reincarnation of the Living Buddha. A soothsayer had outlined a scene to them that directly corresponded to the one taking place outside the gate. At that moment the door of the house swung open and the colonel's wife, carrying a son in her arms of about the same age as the beggar-boy, stepped into the courtyard. Not knowing which boy was the reincarnation of the Living Buddha, the officials took both children off and examined them, finally pronouncing the colonel's child to be the true inheritor.

"Are you the beggar-woman's son?" asked the servant beginning to see the light. Then, in a disappointed voice he continued, "I was asleep when all this was going on. My father didn't dare draw attention to me."

The sage twisted his lips whimsically and stroked the peevish goat's head. Eager to check the validity of his story, the gate-keeper challenged him. He pointed towards the goat and said, "Call him 'brother'."

"Brother!" the sage called out, his senile voice trembling.

"Baaa," responded the goat.

"Now do you believe me?" asked the sage, imploringly.

The animal, with tears streaming down its furry face

at the memory of what it had done in its previous life, confirmed the story by nodding vigorously.

"Now will you tell me who telephones the spinster?" asked the sage, seeing his chance. His other eye blinked.

"He has called every morning for twenty years," answered the servant and then, checking himself, he slapped himself reprovingly on the cheek. "No, I won't tell you." He clenched his teeth.

"Ah." The sage nodded knowingly, but nevertheless still seemed puzzled.

"The young master's dead," murmured the gate-keeper sadly. He turned towards the quiet, empty courtyard with a heavy heart. Slowly he entered, only poking his nose back outside the gate to snap, "Is that also a story about the master? I know that even gods can turn into demons."

Early the next morning the gate-keeper hurried over to open the gate. The corner was deserted. The sage and his goat, after a twenty-year stay, had suddenly disappeared. All that remained was a steaming puddle of piss.

The servant had planned to tell the sage what he knew about the old spinster. It wasn't much, and in fact he had never set eyes on her because she had been sick for a long time and never went downstairs. However, the phonecalls were made by a secret lover. She had never met him, but her life hung on his daily call, and since she had heard from him every day for the last twenty years, when yesterday no call came she had cried and called his name all through the night. Early in the morning she died. The gate-keeper had just this minute discovered that the night before a rat had gnawed through the electric wire on which this human life had so desperately hung.

The servant had also wanted to make sure that everything that had happened the previous day wasn't a dream.

But all he saw was piss: whether done by the old man or the animal he didn't know.

The old man walked three times around the courtyard. Then he spat three times as though exorcising a demon. Trembling, he hurried back to the gate and bolted it, as if he would never open it again.

Translated by Lei Ming

The Old Manor

FISSURES, spreading out like discarded old yak skins, rent the sunbaked earth of the fields at the foot of the mountain. As the sun began its slow descent into the horizon, the peasants simultaneously stopped work and began dragging their exhausted limbs towards home, pulling their ploughs, spades, picks, ropes and animals behind them and leaving a trail of zigzagging furrows in the muddy yellow road. Crows hovered in their wake, hopping around the droppings left by the animals as they moved slowly in the direction of the village. Women carrying triangular willow baskets walked with heads bowed, mechanically twisting the rough leather bands tied around their broad foreheads. Babies, who had been seated all day in the shade of a large rock, either gazing at their mothers or at the blue sky, now sat silently in their baskets; and the setting sun cast elongated, contorted shadows on the road ahead of them.

As commune members, they left for work collectively, took breaks collectively and came home collectively. They knew nothing of what went on in the world beyond the ridge of mountains surrounding the village, though they had heard about a certain "Paris Commune" that had existed in a faraway place a long time ago. To them, it had just sounded like another empty phrase, as meaningless as the concept of Nirvana which had once been explained to them by a lama.

On the outskirts of the village an old man was digging ditches, which he ground out of the stony ground with a spade and his bare, calloused hands. The ditches were full of thick, turbid water and he had spent the entire last few years trying to scoop it out with a broken brass basin. Thus had his declining years been squandered in the futile repetition of a most mindless chore.

The fellow, called Langqin, had once been the first chairman of the village people's commune, but had fallen from grace, charged with a strange, alien crime of which none of the villagers had ever heard, which indeed had been unrecognized by the natives for centuries. He was accused, in short, of being a "corrupt, degenerate element", and had in consequence been sent to this unyielding site to dig the foundation for what was, apparently, to be a storeroom for the commune. So began the ladling of muddy water from a ditch that could never be emptied.

A crowd of commune members passed him by, each of the women looking out at him from under her eyelashes and smiling, their various smiles being gentle, sympathetic, sweet, idiotic, bitter or poignant. They had always loved the man. He had been, until the age of forty-seven, a virgin, but once initiated had slept, over the following ten years or so, with every woman in the village, be she married or single, beautiful or ugly, clever or stupid, buxom or frail, vivacious or sedate, and altogether they had borne him two hundred and thirty-seven daughters, most of whom had died shortly after birth, either due to illness or to some other misfortune. Each daughter was characterized by the presence on her left arm of a single red birthmark in the shape of an eye. Later, in the ancient city of Lhasa, these marks enabled Langqin to recognize them. The one thing these poverty-stricken women had, after all, to be proud of, was their wombs, which were like ever-blossoming flowers that could bear fruit at any time and at any place. So, not only did they bear their husbands' sons and daughters, but they also produced a constant stream of daughters with the red birthmark for Langqin, even after he had descended from being a haughty chairman to a "corrupt, degenerate element".

Passing him now, one or two of the women softly rubbed their protruding bellies and smiled secretively as if to say, "See? Got another one. It's yours."

Old Langqin continued to scoop vacuously. Steeped in water his feet had become soaked white and were rotten to the bone.

A creamy, cool moon slowly rose from behind the mountains until it hung high in the firmament. Full and majestic, it looked like an iridescent antique bowl, now spreading its cold, eerie light on earth and turning the houses, trees and other earthly forms into distorted, seemingly deformed silhouettes. Even the road and mountains seemed misty and remote, and the polished rocks along the roadside glistened with a cold blue light.

Most of the villagers had gone to the district centre to see a film. There was only one show every few months and usually they had seen it before, sometimes indeed they had been seeing the same film for years. Nonetheless everybody went, except the very old and the very young, for whom the three or four-mile walk there and back was prohibitive. These went to bed early. The narrow windows of the stone huts were like black holes.

No light alleviated the darkness, nor could any sound be heard. It was as if the village had long ago been abandoned. Rusty tools littered the threshing ground, and since there was no electricity, and since fuel was in short supply, the threshing machines, sowing machines, winnowing machines and pumps that had at some point been transported here, had never been used, becoming instead as many heaps of useless metal.

Quietly, the moonlight had turned the threshing ground snow-white. Old Langqin lay next to a woman on a tattered straw mat beside the threshing machine, his low, dry cough occasionally echoing through the darkness. The woman's name was Lhamo Quzhen. Once a beautiful but imperious aristocrat, she had been the owner of a mansion with a hundred acres of land. She had moved here from Lhasa after a disastrous love affair and had taken charge of the local manor-house, one of the many properties her family had owned in Tibet. Abandoning her extravagant, somewhat dissolute life in the city, along with its fops and dandies, she had come to live alone and in peace. The years passed and her once youthful maids became sagging old women, though she herself remained elegant and charming; her well-nurtured beauty and natural dignity seemed indeed to crystallize and become timeless, like the holy inscriptions carved on stone tablets. People were dazzled by the agelessness of the once cruel beauty who, by their reckoning, must have been in her late seventies or early eighties.

Now down and out, she was an untouchable,

humbler than a homeless dog. She lowered her head when commune members approached her and, bending over, gazed at her knees while they strutted past.

Even after her fall from grace, men had lusted after her, but every time she slept with one of them he would feel an icy chill running through his limbs the following day; his tongue would feel numb and his body sapped of energy, as though struck with a fatal illness. They said she had the blood of a viper flowing through her veins, and that she was an incarnation of Rakshasa, and that cold air seeped out of her pores. They never dared touch her again.

Langqin and Lhamo Quzhen sat in the darkness and, as he pulled out his tobacco pouch and slowly puffed, both gazed out silently towards one silhouette that dwarfed all others — that of the manor house — for centuries a symbol of power and nobility, and now for want of an owner's care and attention, dilapidated and mournful.

"It used to be mine," murmured old Langqin to himself.

"It was mine," retorted Lhamo Quzhen, her large beautiful eyes flashing indignantly.

"Ah, but I usurped not only your bedroom but the entire house." He laughed dryly.

"Sooner or later I'll move in again. It's God's will," she said, in a voice trembling with emotion.

In his mind, Langqin heard the voice of the district Party secretary who had often said, when he himself had been chairman of the commune, "They want to regain their lost paradise." It seemed so ruthlessly true.

Many years ago Langqin had been one of Lhamo Quzhen's many servants, living in a sunless corner of a basement in the ancient mansion. He was essentially a slave who, due to an unfortunate physical resemblance to the handsome young Lhasa dandy who had deserted her, was forced to bear, by proxy, the brunt of Lhamo Quzhen's rage and revenge. She tortured him. Announcing that he was to be her night-servant, she would lie provocatively in bed and order him to stand by her bedside, while never allowing him to touch her. She would seductively expose her delicate flesh, and while driving him mad with desire, nevertheless forbade him to have any contact with any of the other women in the house. She watched him like a hawk and made certain of his misery by having him chained in iron during the day and thrown into the basement. He bore all this in mute silence — as madly hostile towards his mistress as he was infatuated.

Old Langqin closed his eyes. He suddenly felt giddy, as though circled in a halo of light. As his senses drifted, he felt himself drawn helplessly back into the vortex of the past. Once again he saw in his mind's eye a single shaft of sunlight, shimmering with infinite particles of dust, pierce through the narrow, triangular air-vent of the thick cellar wall and make its seemingly motionless transition from the wall to the crack in the rafter, thus indicating that his mistress was about to rise from her afternoon nap — a respite she took daily, and at length, in her third floor bedroom. Bending low under the thick basement doorway, he moved up the steps, hands brushing against the cold moist wall. Suddenly, as he reached the landing, brilliant sunshine, reflected through a half-open window, dazzled his eyes. Squinting, he washed his hands in the kitchen. Then, taking a delicately-wrought silver basin, he scooped it half full of warm water. He picked up his mistress' perfectly white face-cloth which hung on a wooden stand and put it into the basin which he proceeded to carry up the broad, brass-panelled wooden steps to the third floor. Continuing through a spacious lounge, he stopped on the southern side of the manor in front of a white curtain embroidered with a blue cross. He waited reverently for the sound from inside and soon the bell rang pleasantly and gently.

With servile reverence, Langqin walked deliberately to his mistress' large bed, all the while staring intently at the white face-cloth floating in the basin. But Lhamo Quzhen's ruthlessly flirtatious gestures compelled him to briefly lift his fearful eyes. As he caught sight of her dishevelled dark hair, her half naked, undulating chest, her lasciviously dreamy eyes, her round arms and soft white legs, he clenched his teeth and squeezed his eyes shut, his taut muscles trembling. Overwhelmed with desire, a bitter moan escaped his lips. This, for his mistress, was the most satisfying moment of all.

Langqin's torture ended with the establishment of New China. A crisp gunshot echoed under the blue sky, followed by the sporadic rumbling of cannons and cracking of rifles. None of the staff in the manor knew what was happening; all they saw in the days that followed was a rush of activity: the butler and assorted servants darting in and out carrying spear-guns and swords and fixing yak-skin bags onto the frightened horses. Finally they saw their mistress emerge wearing a red cloak and bearing an expression that was both proud and sorrowful. She stepped over Langqin — prostrate on the ground in front of her — and mounted her horse. Finally she turned slowly towards him and said in a low voice, "Now, you are free."

With that, the gathered horses galloped off in single file in the direction of a desert mountain, leaving behind them nothing but a cloud of dust and yellow sand.

Langqin stood on the stone steps of the empty manor. His heart was void, his head blank. This sudden, unexpected freedom had made him a stranger to himself. He stretched out his arms and pinched his legs but could feel nothing; they seemed to belong to someone else. Eventually recovering his sense, he suddenly dashed into the mansion. The grandiose lounge and luxurious bedroom were in such a state of disorder that it looked as though they had just been looted. The sight of it stimulated his own desire to possess and destroy. Roaring like a lion, he pounced into his mistress' unmade bed, rolling, tearing and biting. He wrapped the smooth silk covers, which he never before dared touch, round his body, breathing in his mistress' aroma like a maniac. Brutally he rubbed his greasy, dishevelled hair on her soft, embroidered pillow. Then, tearing open the pillowcase, he shook the feathers over his head and screwed up the brilliant white bedsheets, already spattered with dark black oil. Eventually springing up, he found for himself a long sword in the downstairs storeroom and rushed to the stables outside the house. There were only a few horses left. He untied the reins of a particularly unruly one, mounted, and beat madly on its loins with his fists. The horse gave a long, shocked neigh and darted out.

Five days later a group of strangers arrived at the manor as though arriving from outer space. They were the reform team and brought with them the breath and flavour of the new era. Just as the manor staff were joyously receiving livestock, farm tools, silver dollars and other items, Langqin, soaked in blood, rode back into town. Tied to his horse was the thinly-clad figure of Lhamo Quzhen. People shouted in surprise.

Langqin never told anyone how he had managed to seize Lhamo Quzhen from her body-guards and servants, but having captured an escaped aristocrat, he had succeeded in turning himself from the most humble of serfs into a local hero. When the members of the reform team asked the destitute hero what he wanted in return, Langqin declared with a cold, savage light in his eyes: "I want to screw Lhamo Quzhen!"

The team was initially shocked, but a few moments later they discovered in his wild cry an extraordinary courage. They admired his mettle which, compared with the timidity of the other villagers, was considerable. They therefore allowed him to do what he wanted without interference.

That night, a beam of silver moonlight flowed through the window into Lhamo Quzhen's battered bedroom, placing the disordered, ghostly-white bed into a kind of spotlight. Langqin's lips, dry and cracked, were flecked with blood and his shoulder ached with pain from a recently sustained wound. Blood surged wildly at his temples, metallic liquid seemed to flow in his ears. In a deadly convergence of despair, fear and bewilderment, he fell on the passive Lhamo Quzhen like a collapsing mountain peak. Her cold-blooded body quivered and her beautiful face twitched in trepidation, giving her an expression which was almost bestial. She fainted under Langqin's vengeful and merciless penetration.

In the tumultuous days that followed, Langqin became not only the leader of the first cooperative team, but also director of the first poor peasants' association and chairman of the first people's commune. In accordance with his status he became the new master of the mansion, moving unceremoniously into Lhamo Quzhen's large, comfortable bedroom. Gazing out of the wall-to-wall window, he realized that he had become the village's most respected citizen. In the early days, while his position was still novel, he continued to work alongside the peasants in the fields, sowing in spring and harvesting under the blazing sun in autumn. Gradually, however, he took to strolling down to the edge of the field and, standing with his hands on his hips, merely observed and supervised. In his capacity as a local official he often attended meetings at the district's centre and would ride off, equipped with a rifle, on the best horse in the village. On his way home he would hunt wild rabbits and pheasants — even, on occasion, coming across wild goat and river deer. Still later, he stopped going down to the fields altogether and spent his days sitting in his bedroom or relaxing on a cushion made of river deer skin in the sun. Lhamo Quzhen's cooks had now become his cooks, her efficient servants, his efficient servants. Like slaves, the commune members provided their master with a continuous supply of butter, beef, mutton, cheese and wine, which tribute they considered his inalienable right. Finally he was living the high life, with wealth, dignity and power, and he began to understand why some people sweated and slaved in the fields all day, their backs peeling under the scorching sun, their hands chapped, while others merely stood aloft on their balconies after a pleasant meal and marvelled at the fresh, tranquil countryside. The attractions of such a position were irresistible, and to actually experience it was like experiencing heaven. Now that they all belonged to him, the mountains, streams, woods, rocks, fields and houses — which had previously seemed to him inert — all took on new life and dimension. Moreover, if he wanted to he could order any commune member to do his bidding at any time, despite the fact that they were not different from him. They, like he, had eyes, hands, sturdy limbs and strong heads.

When night fell, women members would line up at the foot of the stone steps leading up to his mansion and wait to be called. When they later crept out of his room, they each had secreted in their bosom a small piece of butter or meat — the reward given them by the commune chairman for having offered up their bodies. What they never realized was that these fragments were only the dog-ends of what had been handed over to the chairman by their own husbands during the day. They were content. After all, he was a virile young Apollo and they liked him. Furthermore they were grateful for his suckling; gaining his love meant longer breaks for suckling their babies by the fields and more credits on their record books at the end of the year.

They bore him one daughter after another, each with the eye-shaped birthmark on her left arm, and they were proud of it.

Lhamo Quzhen lived in the same low-ceilinged stinking storeroom in the same cracked earthen shack that, along with the mice and fleas, had previously housed her own servants. During the day she carried out the heaviest, most menial tasks and, wandering around like a ghost with a willow-basket strapped to its back, had to endure insults from children and adults alike, all of whom felt free to spit and throw stones at her at random. Her clothes were ragged and threadbare, her appearance unkempt. Only when washing herself in the moonlit stream could she find in her reflection any trace of her former beauty.

One evening, as she was washing, she suddenly felt her hair grabbed by a large coarse hand, which pressed her to the ground. It was none other than the dignified chairman Langqin. She struggled to her feet and, clutching hold of his big, stinking feet, kowtowed repeatedly, moaning: "Oh forgive me! Pardon me! Excuse me!"

The full moon, on the 15th of the lunar month, gleamed like a vast silver bowl. Langqin tore open her clothes and calmly diverted himself with her. He always arrived when there was a full moon, though he was unaware of the fact that nature had adjusted his lust to coincide with the one day in the month — the 15th — on which her blood was warm. God had bestowed on her a mysterious biological cycle which made her blood warm when the moon was round. Thus, Langqin avoided being attacked by the cold air in her body.

Like all Tibetan villagers, Langqin never understood what the red storm of the "cultural revolution" that made its way over from the east was all about. But during the storm Langqin fell from his position and overnight became Lhamo Quzhen's neighbour, both literally and metaphorically. He lived in the smoke-blackened, smelly shack next to hers, and she, together with a few other men and women who were branded "agents", "rich peasants" or "bad elements", were dragged with him onto a small mud stage in the middle of the village square. Here, two men wearing red armbands and smelling revoltingly of cheap tobacco, forced his arms up behind his back until he thought his shoulders would snap. He was made to bow deeply, the humiliation of which sent him almost mad with rage. He had a completely different class background from the others being struggled against. The people from the county centre categorized him as a "degenerate element". He painfully straightened his neck and asked, "What sort of crime is that?"

"It means you are decadent and have slept with too many women," someone beside him explained.

This only made him all the more angry and bewildered. So sleeping with women was a crime, was it? An unforgivable crime! He had never heard of it referred to as such before, neither in the history of his own forefathers nor in any of the traditional social customs or statutes. He was filled with grief and indignation, yet was powerless to defend himself.

Women had adored him as they had adored God, and they had borne him so many lovely daughters, many of whom would grow up healthy, get married and become mothers and grandmothers. What was wrong with it?

He stared stubbornly in front of him, his eyes lighting on a sea of female faces, all of whom were weeping in sympathy.

"Look! Don't their tears simply prove they are the

poor victims of the degenerate Langqin?'' shouted a stranger, dramatically.

Suddenly, from amid the thronging crowds, a multitude of tiny black heads emerged. Girls, some only toddlers, others as old as seven or eight, poured onto the stage, babbling excitedly. "Papa! Papa!" They rushed to his side, enveloping him in a tight circle. The stage was in turmoil as little girls darted to and fro like newly-hatched chicks. The chairman of the rally watched in horror as some of the girls approached him with teeth bared as if to bite him. He started back and rushed off the stage in panic, shouting, "Good Lord, did he really produce all these? It's outrageous! Preposterous!"

Langqin was untied. He caressed the little faces that surrounded him, finding it hard to believe that he had so many daughters. He sat on the ground and tried to gather them all to his breast, laughing loudly and happily.

Ever since then the manor had been empty. The incoming chairman, who was also the Party secretary, was a pleasant, honest, illiterate peasant with large bony hands, who in his wisdom refused to move into the mansion, instinctively sensing that whoever became master of the property was in some way doomed to wretchedness. So the manor became the commune's office and a warehouse for grain, and at night became a cavernous void — so black it could have been something from the underworld.

Time passed, and when set against the backdrop of the eternal, sacred, indomitable Tibetan Plateau, the traumatic events of the time, together with the goals, thoughts and ambitions of the local people, seemed as lightweight and as transient as a summer shower. Nature, mysterious and unfathomable, remained unmoved by the plight of man; the sun, moon and stars still rose inexorably in the heavens; the boundless mountains continued to bask under the same blazing sky and nonchalant white clouds; time continued to move on randomly but inevitably, though seeming not to touch the village which, set deep in the narrow valley, maintained the same appearance it had for centuries. At the foot of the surrounding mountains, a pearly-white beach stretched down to a broad, deep river. The mountains themselves, yellow and constricting, were omnipresent; wave after wave of snow-capped peaks stretched out silently into the distance — eerily glacial under the brilliant sky. They formed a permanent natural boundary within which the small desolate village raised one lonely generation after another, each condemned to contemplate the insurmountable barriers of nature.

Occasionally, Old Langqin would climb to the top of the mountains and, with the gigantic peaks for once not looming above him, he would gaze out over the pure, crystal, silent summits into the cloudless infinitude that was the sky. At such times he would grow chilly about the world, fearful of nature and overwhelmed by a society which cast him down and made him helpless. A perpetual unearthly silence reigned — so deep that you could hear the buzzing in your own eardrums. The world appeared to him colourless, lacklustre and icy. Only an eagle stirred high up in the unbroken heavens, hovering above him and looking briefly down at the unhappy village before beating its wings, accelerating, and soaring off into the distance.

Old Langqin prayed. He prayed to heaven and to the eagle, wishing devoutly that the bird could scoop up his weary, shattered heart and take it to a place protected by God. An unbearable yearning filled his soul, like the echo of a long forgotten song, sonorous and soulful. It seemed to flow out from his mind to a place beyond the lonely mountains, beyond the thin air, the snowy summits and the blue sky to reverberate in places too remote for tangible form. Peasants along the high plateau sang aloud the songs of their forefathers; the sounds of their own voices echoing round the valley being the only indication to them that they did, in fact, exist. The voice in Langqin's head now found release as he burst resoundingly into song. The congealed air trembled. The trembling grew and gathered momentum, releasing a current of air which finally reverberated so forcefully that the peaks of snow began to collapse. A majestic white could covered a corner of the blue sky. An avalanche! A massive river of snow rolled into the valley, turning what had been a sharp abyss into a gentle slope. A moment later a muffled rumble was heard, like the neighing horses of a mighty cavalry.

Another decade or so passed, and one dark dawn, when the moonlight was dim and the birds hadn't the heart to sing, Old Langqin finally and sorrowfully left his village. The crisp morning air was tinged with the warm odour of humanity, which in turn was mixed with the sweetish, rust-like smell of the ageless soil and the fragrance of wild flowers, rocks and ancient timber. He walked to the stony beach by the river where a loyal, meaty-faced boatman waited patiently. Together they pushed the yak-skin boat into the river and jumped aboard. After a few slow circles the little vessel moved downstream and over to the opposite bank.

Old Langqin's hands gripped the thick rattan shipboard covered in yak skin and turned to look back. The mountain valleys in the distance emitted the pale grey glow of morning, and a misty new moon hung high over the manor. A donkey caravan from a neighbouring village plodded slowly along the stony, uneven path at the foot of the mountains, their sleek necks giving off a dark blue sheen.

Oh, the old manor! Langqin shut his eyes in pain. He was bidding farewell to the village in which he had wasted the best part of his life. He was also saying goodbye to the women commune members, now asleep, who had loved him, and to his daughters — too many for him to count: they would grow while they slept, eventually becoming blooming young women. And the ghostly, ageless Lhamo Quzhen — what was she dreaming about?

He was gone. Crossing the river, he tracked over the snowy peaks and made his way to the fabulous, sacred city of Lhasa, leaving the gloomy village to gossip and speculate about him.

Times still passed quietly. But people did not forget about him and talked about him often. Some said he had become a lama in Lhasa's Sera Lamasery, others claimed to have seen him begging in the streets of Balang, while others still maintained he had become a gardener in a new luxury hotel.

The truth was that Old Langqin spent the last moments of his life unaware of where he was. He had woken one day to a hubbub of sound and, opening his eyes, found himself surrounded by a crowd of young girls — some of them fashionable, street-wise city girls; others simply-dressed country maidens. A multitude of faces, beautiful and ugly, swam before his eyes. He saw them roll up their left sleeves and point to a red birthmark, often clumsily and impatiently. It was then that he realized that standing before him were the daughters of his own flesh and blood. Overcome with emotion, his eyes brimmed with tears. Unable to speak, he could only listen as they murmured softly in his ears like singing orioles, the sound affecting him as pleasant yet vague. Amid the murmur of voices he heard someone say that the people's commune in his native village no longer existed, that the temple had been rebuilt on the mountain slope and attracted a ceaseless stream of visitors, that a satellite transmission station had been set up at the county centre, that some villagers had bought TV sets.

His deepest concern was for the homeless Lhamo Quzhen, and he also heard a thing or two about her. She had been rehabilitated and had become a member of the standing committee of the county's Political Consultative Conference. She had moved back into her manor and had become doddering overnight. Her hair had grown thin and silvery, and wrinkles creased her eyes. When she emerged from her front door, supporting herself against a stone wall, people were shocked at her appearance. She had become a senile old woman, not far from her grave.

Like its mistress, the manor looked battered and dilapidated. Weeds flourished in the crevices, and part of the roof had collapsed. The beams and stone walls had begun to rot and crack. God knows, the old manor could have already collapsed in ruins.

Old Langqin closed his eyes slowly, his limbs stiffened, his wrinkled face froze into a strange, indescribable expression which was neither sorrowful nor relieved.

He died.

Translated by Shi Junbao

Invitation of a Century

SANGYI'S heart grew heavy as he saw his kite lose its string in a seesaw battle with other kites, swirl down from the sky and disappear behind a mountain. Like his fate, he didn't know what its final destination would be. Perhaps a lonesome shepherd in a desolate mountain village would find it, or perhaps it would fall into a creek and be picked up by a maiden fetching water with her copper ladle. He never thought the kite, with its two black eyes, would, much later, magically be returned to him. He quickly rewound the long string on the wooden spindle and was in no mood to fly another.

The stray kite reminded Sangyi of his home, a small village hidden in a deep valley flanked by two Buddhist pagodas standing on huge rocks. His uncle liked to stroll to an irrigation ditch skirted by green grass, his hands behind his back and carrying a leather rope, as if he were going to retrieve his livestock. Instead, he would step around the ditch and, in a daze, stare at a nearby watermill. It seemed that the mill held a secret from his past. Sangyi remembered, too, the piercing and monotonous creaks of carts bound for home on the empty mud road.

Sangyi worked in a municipal hospital, where he had many friends. His handsome face and suave manners easily made his friends forget his rural background. Now he belonged to the city and would marry a pretty city girl. His employer would give him a nice apartment, where he would bring up his children and live like other citizens. He would come to enjoy life, which was becoming increasingly colourful.

The season of many festivities had come and he was having a wonderful time. Besides going to the parks, he attended many noisy housewarming parties, baptisms for newborn babies and wedding ceremonies. When Gyayang, his friend and a university lecturer in history, sent him an invitation for his wedding, Sangyi felt pleased. Gyayang had never talked about history with him and had always appeared soulful and melancholy, a rare trait among today's young people of Lhasa, who would either look inanely confident and optimistic, or intimidating, or vacuous.

"Do come," Gyayang wrote in his invitation, "but please don't forget to scrub your neck and soap your hands at least twice. Better wash your smelly feet, too, and change into a pair of clean socks." This revealed Gyayang's lack of humour once again, Sangyi thought, though Gyayang had obviously tried hard to make the postscript sound light-hearted. Reading between the lines it hinted at an inexplicable bitterness and an involuntary compromise of his own fate.

Sangyi had only seen Gyayang's bride once and was impressed only by her flashy clothes. Confident of her mediocre English, she spent all her time accompanying foreigners to local scenic and historic spots and frequenting the gaudy bars in the Lhasa Hotel where she sipped coffee or whisky. Gyayang had fretted that she had been brought up in a family of hereditary aristocrats, who were strict about manners and speech, and he feared she was too high and mighty for him. "But they're getting married. Good for them," Sangyi thought.

Sangyi still wanted to spend a few more years as a bachelor. He didn't want to have to worry about being responsible for any young woman. But attending a friend's wedding was usually fun. There were always endless glasses of beer and various delectable dishes to taste. More importantly, there were charming coquettes who were not only willing to dance but to volunteer toasts, and when everyone was intoxicated, you could ask them to do anything.

Sangyi washed himself thoroughly in compliance with his friend's request and stood in front of a mirror examining himself scrupulously from head to toe. Then he set off, impeccably attired, with a whistle and an envelope, on which he had written his congratulations. Inside he had inserted a 50-yuan bank note as well as several *hadas*.

The wedding ceremony was to be held at the bride's home, which Sangyi had never been to. It should be easier to find than a public toilet__ as long as the general direction was correct. You could tell from the carefully-swept, water-sprinkled front yard, the eye-catching, auspicious lime-white design on the ground before the front door, the snow-white *hadas* hanging on the main gate, the smiling, solicitous receptionists at the door, rows of bicycles and motorcycles, festive men and women darting here and there, and merry music that could be heard from afar. All these would indicate a wedding.

Sangyi was striding briskly down the street when a youth, a neighbour, came by on his motorcycle and invited him for some kebab. Sangyi said he had to go to an important wedding ceremony. His neighbour swallowed hard and warned him not to eat too much, lest he get sick. Soon Sangyi ran into a group of friends who asked him to join them for some sweet tea at a teahouse. When he told them about the wedding, they grew serious and warned him not to get too drunk too quickly, or he would miss the night's fun. "It would be a great pity if you spent the night getting nothing." He tweaked his nose to show he took their advice to heart. A moment later, he saw an old flame on the opposite side of the street. She was shouting at the top of her voice to be heard above the heavy traffic, inviting him to a dance. He shrunk back and darted into the crowd pretending not to hear, fearing she would keep on pestering him.

After walking for a long time and still not finding the place, he began to regret not having ridden his bicycle, which he had thought of doing but then rejected, fearing he would be too drunk to ride it back home. Nevertheless, two wheels made faster progress than two feet.

He remembered the question Gyayang had found so perplexing: why had their ancestors never learned to use wheels for transportation, since for hundreds of years they had likened a man's life to a ceaseless wheel and called it samsara. It was not until 1907, when an eight-horsepower Clement rolled into Tibet through a Himalayan pass, that the natives first saw that what was carrying the pile of iron forward were four round objects made of iron rings, spokes and rubber. The people were flabbergasted.

"Why? Why?" Gyayang had asked, casting his melancholy eyes at Sangyi, who had struggled to reply but couldn't find the words. Gyayang never wanted to talk about history with Sangyi, although he would share one or two anecdotes. Often he couldn't help himself from asking Sangyi medical questions, which the latter couldn't possibly answer.

Sangyi kept going, as if by instinct, musing over his lost kite. Everything seemed like a hallucination, the Garden Road he was walking down, the cars that were shooting past him, the foreign tourists with backpacks and hairy legs, the wild dogs creeping in the shadows of trees by the roadside, the gigantic new buildings, the lamas holding flowery nylon umbrellas.

He remembered a friend once told him that if you looked through two mirrors facing each other you could see infinity. Now he was sensing an infinite bewilderment as if he were standing between two mirrors. The city disappeared behind him, so did the fields in the suburbs. Emerging out of a cloud of mists were boundless mountains that stretched as far as the eye could see. The sun hung high in a bright, azure sky, lengthening the day to eternity. A bird shot by like a meteor above the wilderness and landed far away on a jumble of rocks. Trodden by animals, the path before him wound towards a distant valley, where, deadly bleak and desolate, there was not a sign of life.

Sangyi wanted to leave this savage land. He ran to the foot of the mountains, crossed the valley and saw a small, lonesome, destitute village on a slope in the distance. A boulder-strewn road lay between small plots of fields, beside which stood a *mani* mount, a pile of inscribed stones and a ragged banner drooping in the sunshine of the windless day. There were few trees in the village of low, stone-stacked shacks. The

scene looked both familiar and singular. If there had
been two bright white pagodas on the mountainside at
the back of the village, it could have been his own
home.

A group of brutish peasants stood outside the village. Other villagers poked their heads curiously over
the walls and roofs that were piled with dried yak
dung. A huddle of women were holding out *hadas*,
wheat dippers, time-worn tea pots and wine jars. They
seemed to be waiting for a distinguished guest. The butter design on the spouts had melted in the sun and
dripped onto the ground, staining the dry soil. The
women scooped out chunks of butter which they
pinched and stuck into the spout of the pot.

"Excuse me," said a big-nosed old man walking
out of the crowd, "but are you young Master Sangdu
Gyayang Bandan?"

"No, I'm not," Sangyi answered, startled, for he
had never heard that his friend Gyayang was a master
of any sort with such a title. "I've come to attend
his wedding ceremony. Is it here?" he asked the old
man.

"Wedding ceremony?" the old man shook his
head, puzzled. His eyes rolled like beads.

Some lumpish yet aimiable girls were talking with
the young stranger before them. Sangyi noticed one
had a black mole on her chin and looked restless and
fretful. Sangyi had a bad habit of staring at young
girls, a habit he could never seem to break.

"What's this place?" he asked the old man.

"This is Sangdu Manor, haven't you seen anyone
coming this way?"

"Where's your ... Party secretary?" he faltered.

The old man looked at him, confused.

"I mean, where's the district chairman? So, you don't understand! Are the director of security office or the leader of the militia around?"

"I don't understand what you're talking about," the old man said. "If you're looking for someone who's in charge," the old man continued slowly, "there's only the village head — no one's more important than him here. But he's not here right now. He's gone to the courier's post to receive the young master. "

Sangyi glared at the old man and peered all around him before asking, "How long has the village head been gone?"

"How long? Can't remember clearly. Probably yesterday, or a few days, or a couple of years. Anyway, you see now we're all waiting for him patiently," the old man said, winking at Sangyi and approaching him ingratiatingly.

With a ferocious smell of death and decay spouting from his mouth, he began to introduce the place to Sangyi. Yes, this was Sangdu Manor, our great master Sangdu's property. Sangdu was the name of a prominent family in the sacred city of Lhasa. Hadn't you heard about the family when you were in Lhasa? That was really strange. People said he had twenty-seven manors throughout Tibet. This was certainly a small one since it was situated in such a desolate valley. But the forefathers of the Sangdu family had been born here. The old master had passed away a few years ago. Now the young master, Gyayang Bandan, was in charge. Not long ago, I heard he formed a secret alliance with a group of other young aristocrats and was planning to assassinate the prince regent and to seize the Potala Palace and the Summer Palace. But a renegade reported them and they were all arrested. The government ordered that the Sangdus' offspring never be allowed to attain officialdom at any level, and confiscated all their properties and land. The young master was banished for life.

When the old man noticed Sangyi's eyes open wide with amazement, he led Sangyi by hand to a tiny prison cell newly built on a rocky patch of land outside the village. The prison cell was so small that a person could touch both walls without stretching one's arms and so low it was impossible to stand upright. It was built in a rush by order of the county administrator. The walls were cemented with large rocks, thick and sturdy. A tiny window crisscrossed with thick, iron bars was the only air vent. Sangdu Gyayang Bandan would spend the rest of his life here, with only the barest of hopes that the prince regent would be benevolent enough to grant amnesty. They said Gyayang had a beautiful wife and it was not long since they had married.

"But I've come to attend his wedding," Sangyi said in exasperation.

"Maybe," the old man said calmly, "we've only heard...."

"When did what you've told me happen?" Sangyi shouted. His neck grew scarlet.

"You'll soon see when the young master arrives, really."

"What year is it?" Sangyi asked him in a low voice.

"What year?" the old man thought for a moment, and said, "we country people don't care what year it is, so long as we can count our sheep and know how much grain we are harvesting. That's the most important thing.''

"Oh, no!" Sangyi gave a yelp like a wounded dog, dropped to the ground and clasped his head in his hands. He was the type of person who gave in quickly to adversity and shock. Once he had received a telegram that notified him his sister-in-law, a childhood confidant of his, had been killed in a traffic accident. When he finished reading the telegram, he squatted on the ground with his head in his hands and cried his heart out. A mischievous boy, thinking Sangyi was having a fit, poked him in the side till Sangyi laughed out with tearful eyes and running nose. When the boy saw the telegram on the ground and read it, he was flabbergasted and fled like a rabbit, yelling a string of sorries behind him. After crying a little more, Sangyi quietened down and wiped his face.

Holding his head, he shouted a few more times and felt better — so relieved that not a trace of frustration was left in his heart. He asked no more questions, nor nor did he think — there wasn't any reason to think. He accepted the reality peacefully and silently. He took a deep breath, plucked up his courage and walked to the village as if on air. He joined the women villagers and, like everyone else, waited for the guest from afar to arrive. Soon the women stopped casting curious glances at him and seemed to forget there ever was a young man wearing a red shirt with a pointed collar and a pair of jeans and holding in his hands a roll of *hada*. All their attention was focused on the arrival of Sangdu Gyayang Bandan, once the highest man in the area and now a humble prisoner, though they had never seen him. For the villagers, no matter what crime their master had been accused of, he would remain always their awesome master.

The women's faces had been baked scarlet in the blazing sun; their foreheads glared with oil. The fact that the wine in the jars and the tea in the kettles had long gone sour in the sun and in their warm embrace did not bother these women, who only patiently and repeatedly patched the spouts of the containers with new butter designs.

Even the silent, endless mountains seemed crystallized under the glaring, cloudless sky.

Sangyi grew restless as he waited and he swept his eyes here and there at the women. Furtively, he moved closer to the woman with the black mole, who was cradling in her arms a tea kettle as if it were her son. He asked in the gentlest of voices, "Are you tired, maiden?"

"No, no."

"What is your name, maiden?"

"Yamjin."

"What a nice name," he complimented in a low voice and twisted his body around so he could continue their conversation. But she said no more, not even turned to face him. Sangyi was disappointed. He poked her soft waist with a finger and pinched her shoulder gently. She paid no attention. When he saw a loose patch on her pink undershirt, he tore it off mischievously. Under the patch on her delicate white skin was tattooed "Don't touch me" in black. Sangyi covered his eyes with his hands and cowered in shame. He didn't dare to take liberties with her again. Then he realized that beneath her shabby clothes and unwashed skin she hid an angelic beauty and dignity.

Thus, the villagers stood waiting patiently and without a word of complaint. Time could not measure this long, unending respite. The villagers began to age before his eyes. He turned round and found all the young girls, who had been whispering about him, had become old and doddery. They looked at him blankly. He felt his face and heaved a sigh: he too had aged. He'd grown a moustache. He pulled out a few hairs and saw they were white or grey. He moved his waist and feet and heard creaking sounds from inside his joints, like a weathered wooden door on worn hinges.

A sage-like old man had ridden by on a donkey as the villagers waited and he felt he should have gone with him.

A little black spot, a shepherd, appeared on a distant mountain peak. He seemed to swirl his hands, waving at the villagers. A moment later a whistle, feeble yet melodious, was carried across the crystal air — the sentry shepherd was sending a message to his fellow villagers.

"He's coming!" The villagers were thrown into a hullabaloo of excitement. Sangyi was intrigued too, and like everyone else, stood on tiptoe and strained to look towards the serpentine path in the empty valley.

A dark figure emerged from behind a mountain ridge and strode forward, clouds of dust trailing behind him. When people finally realized it was only a white-haired, white-bearded, scrawny old man bouncing on a galloping grey donkey towards them, everyone looked disappointed. They were surprised that the donkey could

run so fast and that the old man could endure jolts
and jerks. Judging from his only possession, a sack on
his back, and his carefree and dissolute appearance,
some villagers concluded that the old man was a min-
strel, some a moonstruck romanticist, some a roaming
Buddhist monk, and some a rustic magician. Inanely,
the old man called himself Sangbe Dondrup the Rover
and said he had roamed and preached all over Tibet to
enlighten benighted peasants.

The villagers thought he was going to show them the
treasures or curiosities inside his sack, but he did
not even touch it. Instead he started describing the
kaleidoscopic world beyond the land of snows in a
style called "zhega", which was peculiar to the peasants. In a typical prologue he offered a eulogy and
prayers to the gods up in heaven and gave greetings to
the folks down on earth. Then he began to tell his
stories exuberantly and eloquently, gesticulating with his
hands and feet: he had crewed on a pirate ship on the
Atlantic; he had flirted with a beauty of mixed blood
under a palm tree in fruit-fragrant Havana; he had witnessed thousands of Muslims praying in unison in
Mecca, Saudi Arabia; he had drunk hot cocoa at the
home of a railway signalman in wintery woods of
white birch in Finland; he had survived scarlet fever in
an African jungle; he had sneaked into the ranks of
striking automobile workers in Detroit and had clashed
with the police; he had lost two ribs in Lhasa's
Drepung Monastery when set upon by a angry crowd
after he had said Cologne Cathedral had an equal gran-
deur.

To make himself understood, Sangbe Dondrup
stripped himself stark naked and danced around and

likened parts of his body to a world map. "Here is the Mississippi River." He felt his spine. "By the way, it's the longest river in the world. And here's the plain of black Africa." He patted his brown and flat stomach. "This is Arabia." He pinched his ear. "And here's Lake Baikal." He lifted his eyelid, "Look how deep it is!" Then he pointed to his crotch and said, "This is the famous Grand Canyon in the state of Arizona, America. And here's the Sahara." He touched his back. "This is the tropical jungle in South America," he concluded, pointing to the black hairs between his legs.

He stopped, thirsty and gasping. The villagers looked at him vacuously. Nobody offered him wine or tea. He shook his head and mumbled, as if cursing under his breath. Why was it everywhere he went he met people who were ignorant, stupid and bereft of knowledge of the world outside? He put on his clothes and dejectedly mounted his donkey. He called out with all his might, "Follow me! Follow me to roam and see the world. My donkey can carry one more person, no more."

"No, we don't want to go!" the villagers shouted back in chorus. Sangyi stuck out his chest and, as if he were also a member of the village, stared at the crazy old man with disdain. The old man left, crestfallen. Even his donkey seemed dejected.

When finally Sangdu Gyayang Bandan and his escort appeared in the distance, it proved to be quite an anticlimax. Marching in front of him were two government soldiers, each carrying a heavy homemade rifle that jerked back and forth on their saddles, and each had a long pigtail that dangled like a black rope from the back of their heads. Following them was a haughty, meaty-faced messenger, who was carrying a parcel of mail tied with a yellow ribbon. He wore a top hat with a broad brim, customary among caravan drivers, and had a long stone earring in one ear. The tall, skinny, village head walked behind, wearing formal clothes and a small red cap like a little bowl. Exposed from one of his sleeves of his gray gown was a section of a leather whip, an emblem of his modest authority. A horse carried two yak-skin bags, possibly the belongings of the banished young master. Keeping abreast was another horse, which carried nothing on its back.

However, to everyone's amazement, they did not see the young master they had long been expecting. Only after the escorts had all dismounted did the villagers notice that the village head was holding in his hands a naked baby and was mumbling with embarrassment, "Oh no, it's terrible! I don't like this at all."

As soon as he got off his horse, the proud messenger loudly asked for wine. A government official to be treated with care, he had the privilege of enjoying free horse rides, food and lodging wherever he went. He took a sip of the wine a woman offered him, only to spit it out at her face, cursing at the top of his voice, "How dare you treat me like a beggar with this sour wine! Get me good wine!" After another woman presented him with another bowl of wine, he only drank half bowl before pouring the rest on the ground, shouting, "Bah! This wine is as bland as water! Get me good wine!" When the third bowl was served, he downed it with one gulp, narrowing his eyes and humming in satisfaction. Immediately he opened his eyes wide again and asked threateningly, "Where've the young girls gone? Why are you staring at me like that, so old and ugly! Don't you have some younger women here? Go and find me a few!'' The women looked at each other in confusion, unable to tell who looked younger.

"Excuse me, is there any mail for me?'' Sangyi, plucking up his courage, asked the messenger.

"What, mail?'' the messenger blinked in bewilderment. ''Here's a land of hungry ghosts, who would send letters here? I would never have come here if not for having to escort the banished convict. Hey, you don't look like a local.''

"No. I'm a lost stranger.'' Sangyi replied in despair.

With no sight of the young master, the villagers surrounded the village head and humbly inquired of him where he was. The village head held up the baby and stuttered what the messenger had told him to say. On the seemingly endless trek from Lhasa, the young master, Sangdu Gyayang Bandan, had been moaning and sighing all the time. He often shed tears, mourning the brevity and transience of life, and wishing that he had not been born and that all that had happened had been only a dream. He shrivelled and shrank slowly. His face became childish and mischievous, like a boy's. One moment he cried for food and complained that riding the horse all day had hurt his bottom, the next moment he cried he was homesick. Thus, he turned gradually from a adult to a small child and, later, from a small child to a baby too tottery to sit by himself on the horse, so the messenger had to carry him in his arms. The three escorts had suffered greatly because of the baby who, according to the messenger, would keep on shrinking until he became a foetus and entered a woman's womb. This brought a chill to all the women, who folded their legs tightly, fearing it would be them the foetus would try to enter.

"He's like a heavy rock," the village head said ruefully, looking first at the baby and then at the forlorn prison outside the village. Nobody volunteered to take the little thing over to it.

"Oh, he's defecating!" someone shouted. The village head looked down and saw a patch of yellowish sludge on his chest. Disdainfully, he laid the baby in a trough in a stable.

Lying in the trough lined with wheat stocks and peas, the baby opened his shiny black eyes and looked at the puzzled villagers, who had clumped together, too fearful to take a close look at him. Silently, they looked at their shrunken young master with awe and disappointment, sympathy and amusement.

Sangyi knew that this must be his old pal, so he forced himself to approach and examined him carefully, trying to enlarge him to his full size in his mind's eye. True, this was his old friend, Gyayang Bandan. An old man and a baby now, they faced each other silently, as always, which was peculiar to men.

"I'm so sorry, Sangyi. I shouldn't have invited you," Gyayang said a moment later with a familiar voice.

"I was lost. I couldn't find your wedding place."

"Nobody did. She emigrated to Canada with a foreigner and settled down there."

"Oh," Sangyi was stunned for a moment. "I've just learned that you're a young aristocrat in exile."

Gyayang's delicate face showed a deep bitterness.

"That happened in my previous life, but people still remember it. I don't know whether it's a good thing or not. The banishment of our Tibetan aristocrats was as moving and tragic as the banishment of the Russian Decembrists. Only few people know about it."

"Why do you have to be like this? Why do you diminish yourself?" Sangyi asked.

"I want to live in a time without any aristocrats. After fifty years I want to be born into this world again. Perhaps it will be a better world then."

"Well, you've shrunken and I've aged," Sangyi said with a long sigh. He wanted to blame him, comfort him, and give him sympathy at the same time, but he felt it was no use. He was about to pat his friend's shoulder when he realized there was hardly anything to pat. All he could do was tap Gyayang's soft bottom, which was marked with purple flecks. Standing quietly aside, he watched Gyayang's body, continue to condense until his hands and feet clutched together tightly and he was covered with lovely folds and his eyes closed tight as if glued shut. Lying on the trough, Gyayang was now a complete foetus. Sangyi knew that his friend was soon to leave him for good.

The foetus started groaning in agony.

Sangyi left him and walked to the villagers. "He wants to get in, don't you understand? Can someone help him?"

Gloomy and ugly, none of the old women dared to take a step forward.

When Sangyi caught sight of the girl with the black mole on her chin, he could not believe his eyes. She was still as young as ever, the only young girl in the whole village now.

She stood silently, then went to the stable, while the others gaped. She bent down to look at the tiny creature, then lifted her skirt and a leg courageously, squatted, and sucked the foetus inside her.

Sangyi turned to look to the remote mountains, forever aloof, the snow-capped peaks glaring under the blue sky. So the young girl, Yamjin, must be the incarnation of Gyayang's mother.

But how could he be linked to Yamjin without an umbilical cord? Sangyi mused. Just then, from behind, a long bitter scream broke the silence.

Yamjin feebly stepped out of the stable. There was no sight of the foetus in the trough. People bent their heads and made way for her, humbly. One villager handed her a stick, another gave her a wooden bowl and still another tossed her worn clothes. Goddess or witch, people would never touch her again and she would leave the village and be a roamer.

It was only when a crowd of people grabbed his arms and tugged him towards the cell that Sangyi felt he was in danger. It was perhaps natural that the villagers should choose him to be a substitute for his friend, who had vanished, for nobody dared to be responsible for leaving the prison cell empty.

"What are you doing? I protest! I will lodge an appeal!" Sangyi shouted, struggling to break away. But no one understood what he was shouting about and all thought him hysterical.

Sangyi was shut up in the cell. Several old women took turns to watch him, providing him with food and tea. In the darkness Sangyi congratulated himself on not having children. Again he thought of Yamjin, remembering that she had gone in the same direction as the mad old man. He wished the old man had been waiting for her, since he had said he could carry one more person on his donkey. One day she would return with her eternally young body, which would represent an even more beautiful map of the world. Perhaps by then the villagers would understand what she was to explain. Sangyi was quite confident of it.

He looked through the air shaft and saw a kite marked with two black eyes falling from the sky. Ah, that was the kite he had lost over Lhasa. He had made it himself. It skirted across the top of the weeds and landed gently on the grass. Several children ran towards it.

"Quick, please! I beg you, pick up the kite for me, please!" he called out anxiously to his guards.

Lifting up their skirts, the old women dashed out as if they had heard a bugle call to charge. Sangyi closed his eyes; he did not have the heart to watch the kite being torn to pieces as the old women and children struggled to retrieve it.

"Young master, I … I've got it!" an old woman said outside the air shaft, panting for breath.

Translated by Shi Junbao

The Light on the Cliff

THE official banquet in the open air was very grand. Its guest was a thin, wretched-looking man of forty. He wasn't an important official or an artist, but everyone addressed him respectfully as "Mr Doctor". People said that the reason his property was worth a million dollars was due to the fact that he had four arms, two of them concealed on his back and stomach. All the officials, including the highest administrator and military commander, surrounded him deferentially. I had no idea why I was there. No one came to question me so I just hung around. The banquet was held on a platform on the top of a grandiose building. Even though a huge sunshade had been set up over the seats for the distinguished guests, shafts of sunlight still slanted onto their faces. In front of them were tables piled high with all sorts of things to eat and drink, and there was a row of beautiful dancing girls. Mr Doctor stood there arrogantly. He cast an indifferent glance over the dancers, then inclined his head to listen to the highest administrator's *sotto voce* flatteries. I stood some way off, and with surprise discovered that my long shadow had fallen across Mr Doctor's face. I felt strangely perturbed and had a sudden sense of forboding — this was sheer blasphemy. He was sure to take offence. Just as I expected, two strong men in Western suits came over and asked me what I was doing there. I knew at a glance that they were Mr Doctor's bodyguards. I had heard that he owned a private squad of them. All of them had received special training at the police academy and were capable of seeing through any disguise. They were constantly around Mr Doctor, protecting him, and they had contemptuously demonstrated their doubts about the protective capabilities of the local police. I couldn't give these two gentlemen satisfactory answers and they pulled me aside. They questioned me again and, finding nothing suspicious, asked me to remove a railing on the edge of the platform. I didn't dare say any more, picked up the tools and set to work. The railing was actually painted on a long piece of cloth and looked like a real one. I used a knife to cut a long strip and pulled it right down to the bottom. Unfortunately a white horse was standing there holding the edge of the canvas tightly in its teeth. I scratched the corner of its mouth and the railing fell down with a thud. Some bodyguards rushed forward, propped the railing up and with great effort carried it away. The horse must be Mr Doctor's, I thought. If anyone noticed that I had injured it I would be in really big trouble. Cautiously, I moved forward, and examined its mouth carefully. It didn't appear to be injured and there was no blood, and the horse merely gave me a hard stare. I heaved a sigh of relief. Standing on the edge of the platform was like standing on the edge of a precipitous cliff. Leaning forward and looking down, I saw a dense crowd of people who were looking up, and who, quite unaccountably, screamed at me.

My wife would not let me appear lonely or ill at ease on such an occasion and came over to keep me company. She was a dignified woman and words fail to describe how much we loved each other. She tucked her arm into mine and we walked ostentatiously past the distinguished guests, like any lady and gentleman. I didn't know whether it was because my shadow had swept across their faces for the second time, but I knew they were displeased. Then I discovered that a number of layabouts had squeezed in. The only reason that the policemen and the bodyguards didn't recognize them was because they were dressed in decent clothes, and were sitting there quietly amongst all those high officials. They had come here simply to sample the dignity of man. And precisely for that reason, even my girlfriend had come. She was mixed in with a group of aristocratic women, and was dressed like a journalist; two cameras slung over her shoulder and a pocket tape-recorder in her hand. She was just an ordinary typist in a company but had somehow come to appear rather sexy. She had always wanted to be a journalist, even in her dreams. When she saw me, she waved a journalist's greeting. We had met each other in a deserted street on a winter's night. Of course my wife knew that she was my new girlfriend and that I liked her, but she never interfered in my private life, knowing that this side of things had never affected the feelings we had towards each other.

"Hey! How about my skills?" asked my girlfriend.

"Not bad."

I knew that she was asking me about her skills in bed, and I felt fine about them. Seeing my wife's arm tucked in mine, she looked rather confused and hurt. My wife and I walked into an empty rest room, sat down on a long sofa and held each other tight, sensing wave upon wave of happiness and tranquillity. Then I noticed my girlfriend. She stood in the door way, like a child who has been neglected and wronged. Affectionately I beckoned her over. She pursed her lips, walked over and sat down beside me. I fondled her thigh aimiably, discovering that she was more beautiful and lovely than ever. When was the last time we had met? "When I go back to work," she said while I was thinking hard, "I will tell the manager that I went to the West last month to gather news."

She had always pictured herself as a journalist. I finally recollected the last time I had seen her. It was a rainy day; the building of the company she worked for had collapsed in torrents of rain; I was watching from afar under an umbrella when people dug her body out of the pile of muddy ruins; her head was hidden by the rescuers who were carrying her, so I only saw her bloated, white hand dangling and swaying, and the blood dripping from her body. I was afraid to look at the dead, so I covered my face, turned and ran away.

"I'm terribly sorry," I said. "I fell ill on your funeral day."

"No, that's not true," she said unhappily. "I was doing an investigation and collecting material along a river. The helicopter was tossed about in the turbulence so that I was asleep one moment and awake the next. It was an unpleasant feeling. Later, I was conscious of nothing."

I didn't want to say anymore, so I turned and looked out of the window. She chatted animatedly with my wife, their hands clasped together, but I was in no mood to listen. The valleys in the distance were surging with a raging tide as if torrents of water had rushed down the mountain. I was struck with awe by this grand sight, and my eyes, like zoom lenses, drew its distant scene close and clear: thousands of wild oxen and deer were fighting down the mountainside, churning the earth right up into the sky above; the deer were dying in countless numbers and were impaled high on the horns of the oxen, and then, as soon as they were hurled down to the ground, trampled into meat pies. They crushed and squeezed themselves together and the weak exerted their utmost feeble strength to ward off attack, yet were still swept away; they rolled down in a tangle of fighting, and behind them the ground was densely covered with the bodies of oxen and deer.

"Darling!" A soft, sweet voice rang out behind my ears. For a moment, I was unable to make out who was calling, my wife or my girlfriend. I loved them so much.

I turned round. The two strong men in Western suits walked towards me with gloomy expressions.

"Why can't you leave me alone?" I shouted impatiently.

"You have stabbed Mr Doctor to death," one voice said icily.

"Me?"

"Yes. Your shadow."

"You," my wife rebuked lovingly. "Others are much nearer to Mr Doctor but *they* didn't cast their shadows on him. Look at yourself."

I stepped out of the door, stood in the sun and sure enough, saw that my long shadow had reached the end of the row of houses. I had nothing to say. My girlfriend blew me a kiss and waved the tape-recorder in her hand, signalling that she had to do an interview and go. I felt clear-headed. I knew that she had died two months ago and what appeared now was merely her ghost that had failed to realize her dreams of becoming a journalist. When my eyes were caught by the glinting of the iron handcuffs which had been put on my wrists, I thought of a line from the Old Testament: ''God said 'Let there be light and there was light' .''

So there had been this damned shadow.

"It's unfair!" I said to my wife before I was taken away by the two toughs.

"My dear," she said loudly with tears in her eyes. "Take the injustice and misery of this world with you. Let them go to hell!"

Translated by Wang Ying

The Banished Prince

ONE late afternoon, when the wind was blowing a gale, Prince Gunsa arrived in the town of Luoda, to where he had been banished. The carriage driver and soldiers escorting him unloaded the little luggage he had in the town-square and then hurried off, disappearing in a cloud of yellow dust. It was as though he'd been left behind in a ghost town. The houses were all closed up, the street was deserted and there wasn't even a stray dog to be seen. The howling wind sent clusters of tumble-weed whizzing by his feet and in the dust the houses with their faint silhouettes appeared unreal.

When it was almost dark, a man appeared who took him to an elderly woman's home. Her name was Nganini and she lived alone, so Gunsa moved into her house. His outlandish city clothes and high-class hairstyle were no longer appropriate, so at Nganini's advice he visited the tailor, Melung, who made him a suit of black woollen clothes, the same as those worn by the people of Luoda. His jacket was short and if he raised his arms his belly showed. It had a firm, upright collar and was fastened on the left by two brass buttons — one near his armpit and one high up on the chest near his neck. The chest, collar and sleeve-cuffs were all embroided in gold. Later, the blacksmith, Ngadin, gave him the same basin-style haircut common to the men in Luoda Town. He went home, took one look in the mirror and almost fainted, thinking he couldn't look any more ridiculous or local than this.

As a result, the folk of Luoda no longer took him for an outsider and Melung's daughter, Yonna, subsequently fell in love with him.

At dusk, Gunsa and Yonna would stroll arm in arm down the one and only street in Luoda until they reached the old walnut tree at which point they would return. Yonna was very beautiful and had a heart of gold. She really felt for Gunsa and hearing of his misfortunes would make her weep.

"It's nothing, my father was also banished," he said.

"I know, my grandfather told me."

"But the townsfolk didn't like him, so they may also dislike me."

"It's just that they don't know how to make friends with outsiders."

"How did you manage?"

"I don't know."

Luoda was dead quiet and, when free, people had nothing better to do than sit around on the doorsteps or lie back against the wall, close their eyes and bask comfortably in the sun. After talking about this, Gunsa and Yonna felt it was their responsibility and duty to stimulate the young people's enthusiasm and desire to improve. Not long afterwards a sign was placed above Nganini's door: "Youth Hostel". Gunsa gathered the youngsters around and turned on the small radio he had brought with him. They listened to the broadcast but what they heard had nothing in common with their own lives and they gradually lost interest. Gunsa then suggested he teach them some songs. He sang *Old Man River*, *Katusha* and *The Green*, *Green Grass of Home*. The youngsters also sang a few songs which were either vulgar or simple children's songs, passed down through the generations.

When free, apart from saying arbitrary prayers to the goddess, Boko, the only other thing of interest was to await the great one.

In the mountains to the north of Luoda there was only one temple. It was called Lhakang Temple and had a great lama who many years before had gone to the mountain caves to practise Buddhism. He had the amazing ability of being able to manifest himself in many different forms. He would frequently transform himself into a huge red eagle and soar into the skies above Luoda until he disappeared behind the mountains. His awesome cry was beyond the comprehension of the townsfolk and it seemed as though all the houses in the small town were shaking.

The lama's ability was, indeed, amazing and Gunsa witnessed with his own eyes the wonderous spectacle of the lama flying above. He, too, felt the earth tremble but was not in the least bit surprised. But the residents of Luoda were not in the least bit surprised at his lack of surprise.

At night, the people of Luoda would go to bed very early and there was no light or sound. When Gunsa couldn't sleep he would wander around the town-square. The clear, cold moonlight cast a silvery white light upon the ground and he saw his ghost-like shadow tangled around his feet. The more he looked the more ghastly and terrifying it became. Finally, he fled and returned to Nganini's.

"That year I waited upon his Lordship in this house. Now, again, I must wait upon his son. I'm willing to bet that in another twenty years I may still have to wait upon his grandson ... that's if I'm still alive!" she would prattle on and in her complaints there was a touch of pride.

"I'm willing to bet, granny, that I'll be the last aristocrat in my family line to be banished."

"Ultimately isn't it Boko who decides?"

She swayed as she climbed into bed, undid her sash and her baggy black dress which hung over her feet and looked like a roc spreading its wings. Just before bedtime she would face west, bowing fully prostrate three times. In the lamplight her dark shadow would move up and down on the clay wall like a demon doing a strange kind of dance. Seeing, this gave Gunsa the creeps and he would hide under the bed covers, quietly turn on his radio and randomly tune into stations from the countless frequencies in the night sky. One moment he listened to the variety show on the BBC, another, a magazine show on VOA and the next, the international news on Radio Moscow....

"My boy, is that a mouse you have there under the covers? Ee ee ee, ee ee ee, it sounds as if it's about to give birth," Nganini said in the darkness, turning over with a thump.

"This mouse can't give birth, it just wants to tell me some interesting stories."

"Oh, then it must be a male."

He tuned in to the radio station in Lhasa and the voice of the woman reading the news sounded familiar. He tried hard to think back to his dissolute days there and wondered whether or not he knew her:

"Planes from ... this year have constantly violated our country's air space. Regarding this matter, a spokesman from the Ministry of Foreign Affairs issued the following statement...."

The radio signal was very weak and the broadcast could only be heard intermittently because of the static.

" ... and a strong protest has been lodged."

One day, some mountain dwellers came running into town reporting that, while they were out herding, they had seen a foreign couple, carrying a baby on their back, and accompanied by a border tribesman, who seemed to be acting as their interpreter, and several horses, heading this way. After many years of peace, the town of Luoda was sent into an uproar by this news. They were duty-bound to resist the encroachments of foreigners and it was a rare occasion for ceremony and pleasure. In the past, their ancestors, on many occasions, had successfully contained all types of foreign invaders, both adventurers and spies, on the far side of the Marqu River, outside the town, forcing them to turn back.

These achievements had long ago become legend and stirred people's hearts. But, there was a time when a foreign army of hundreds, equipped with awe-inspiring guns and cannons, facing countless tribesman, villagers and town-dwellers, men and women alike, who had gathered in their thousands brandishing swords to defend their homeland, marched defiantly into Lhasa. This humiliating event had been erased from the town's memory.

Soon afterwards, the dust began to fly, the dogs howled, the horses whinnied and the townsfolk let out their war cry as though they were exorcising demons.

The men went off to ransack the cluttered storerooms, searching high and low, even in the clay ovens, for weapons. Some of the old swords they found had rusted in their scabbards and couldn't be drawn. All they could do was fasten the scabbards to a tree trunk and tie one end of a leather rope to the pommel of the swords and the other to the tail of a horse. The men let out a shout, each giving his horse a slap on the rump which sent the horses galloping off, thus pulling the swords from their scabbards. A quick glance was sufficient to reveal that the swords had corroded in their scabbards leaving only half the sword, and the women cried out.

From ancient legend they had learned what was appropriate behaviour for women before the men went off to battle. The women would offer up wine to the stern-faced soldiers on horse back, constantly worrying that their men would become intoxicated and fall from their horses. When the men were about to set off, the women would tightly clutch the reigns of her husband or lover's horse. Before the women would let go the men had to lash their loved one several times with their whips, hit them with the back of their swords or kick them. Even this wasn't sufficient, and it wasn't until they'd been dragged for a distance behind the galloping horse that they were forced to let go. Crawling along the ground they would gesture towards the horses in the distance, shouting:

"Brave men, Boko will ensure your victory and safe return!"

A motley band gathered on the banks of the Marqu River to defend the small log bridge which was the only way intruders could gain access to the town from

outside its gates. When a few people and several horses
emerged on the sand flats at the foot of the mountain
on the opposite side of the river, the soldiers' composure stiffened with the advent of battle.

The town chief was a pacifist who wanted to choose
two people who would pluck up enough courage to
cross the bridge and negotiate with the intruders. When
the tailor, Melung, was chosen it was discovered that
he was nowhere to be seen among the crowd. The people couldn't believe that he could be so cowardly as to
shirk his duties at this most critical juncture. Needless
to say, the worldly Gunsa from Lhasa satisfied the
chief and became his representative.

The intruders were a European couple carrying a one-
year-old baby boy. They claimed they had come to see
the sacred mountains and lakes and to go to Lhasa to
pay their respects and had no other motive — political,
military or otherwise.

The chief delegated Gunsa to go over and through
their interpreter negotiate with the adventurers. He was
to explain that if they allowed them to go, the authori-
ties in Lhasa would severely punish the residents of
Luoda and, for this reason, they could not allow them
to go on, they must request permission from officials in
Lhasa.

The baby being carried on the back of one of the
Europeans aroused great curiosity and tenderness
among the townsfolk and they gradually crowded
around. The baby boy with his soft golden locks, blue
eyes, turnup nose and soft skin brought constant
sighs among the audience. They'd never seen such a
strange or beautiful child before. He was like a small
bodhisattva descended from heaven. One after the

other they reached out, lightly stroking his cheeks. The child seemed to have inherited all the composure of a European gentleman; he didn't cry or moan but merely opened his small mouth, smiling and nodding his head repeatedly at the strangers gathered around him. Soon his cheeks were shiny with grease from all the hands rubbing his face.

One person suggested exchanging five head of yak for the child to which his father repeatedly shook his head. The people pointed out that if they went to other places they must be careful as there were people who would look at the child the same as they would a pedigree pug-dog and want to steal him. But you could be reassured as there were no thieves here. Before they realized it the European couple were already on the bridge. Someone let out a shout and everyone suddenly noticed. Stern-faced they raised their swords forcing the couple back off the bridge.

That night the European travellers set up camp on the sandy river bank. What followed were endless rounds of talks. Every day Gunsa would cross the river with the chief and jabber on with the Europeans who possessed amazing patience and strength of purpose. They discussed a wide range of topics: from the interests of their two countries to their system of beliefs, looking at the lessons of history, then moving on to the special nature of the Holy city and then back to the interests of their two countries again. Whenever they finished they would find they had gone right back to where they had started from. It was just like a never-ending cycle.

Gunsa couldn't bear doing nothing but jabber, so he brought a shaggy English rug from home and unravelled it, combed it out and then rolled it into a ball. Afterwards, he would twist the wool while carrying out the negotiations. The Europeans greatly admired the young bumpkin local's eloquence. The man said:

"You're a born diplomat, why doesn't your country take more notice of your talent instead of allowing you to waste your life away in this backward place?"

"Sir, please note that I am not from these parts. I am an aristocrat who has come here in exile."

"Very interesting," the man exclaimed, adding excitedly, "this makes me more curious and determined than ever. I'm definitely going to Lhasa to see its secrets."

"I understand your determination completely, just as I feel curious about the mysteries in your country. But...."

Gunsa basically couldn't remember what he'd been talking about. He'd only been going through the motions, subconciously, using language which was flawless and appropriate to the occasion. He was only concerned with twirling the wool in his hands evenly and could think only of Yonna. That day in front of her he'd severely criticized her father for his deplorable behaviour. She didn't know how to justify her father and only cried silently.

But nobody, including Gunsa and Yonna, knew that Melung was currently working on a secret weapon. There was a tattered fragment from an ancient sutra which he'd obtained by chance from a man meditating in a cave ten years earlier. The sutra was called: "Mysterious and Profound Sutra for Manufacturing Divine Weapons of Fire and Brimstone to Subdue

Karmic Obstructions Throughout the Three Realms. "
For more than ten years he'd absorbed himself
in studying the mysterious words of the sutra and
pondering over its difficult formula and amazing il-
lustrations. His ultimate aim in attempting to manufac-
ture this powerful, murderous weapon was not for use
against intruders. He had his reasons but couldn't tell
anyone.

Gunsa and Yonna loved each other, but not being
able to make love to her irritated him. She always re-
sisted his advances. Besides, she knew that if they had
a baby he might never get to return to Lhasa. But
Yonxi, the elder daughter of Melung, satisfied Gunsa's
sexual urges and without any hitches. She was a beautiful, easy-going girl and they would make love every
night, rolling around together, in the cowshed at the
back of Nganini's house. But they didn't love each
other and this satisfied Gunsa very much.

The days passed and the flying lama still frequently
appeared in the skies over the town. Autumn arrived,
and the strong winds began to blow. The villagers regu-
larly gathered at the bridge outside the town carrying
their weapons and looking the part to the European
adventurers who had long overstayed their welcome
and who had no plans to leave. Gunsa, acting as the
town's sole delegate, would cross the river each morning to negotiate and exchanging mutual greetings he
was just like one of the inhabitants dwelling along the
banks of the Marqu River.

The Europeans would invite him into their tent, and
the topic of discussion would range from the problem
of whether they would be allowed to carry on, to the
American presidential elections, the Olympic Games,

the history of Buddhism, the great masters of the
European Renaissance, the unstable international situation, the lives of African natives. Gunsa also learnt to
speak English and French.

When he'd finished twisting the wool he asked
Yonna to make a thick hard blanket. With his hands
free he felt ill at ease so he unravelled the blanket and
started all over again. At dusk, he and Yonna would
stroll through the town. When night came the peaceful
town could hear the moans and groans of Gunsa and
Yonxi. Gunsa would never forget the image of
Nganini's dark shadow on the wall as she carried out
her bedtime ritual. The batteries in his radio eventually
ran out and Nganini slept soundly, no longer hearing
the sound of mice.

Soon winter would be here. The European travellers,
who had lived on the other side of the river and had
negotiated with the locals for more than half a year,
had completely lost confidence and patience. The mountain passes would soon be sealed by snow and if they
didn't leave in time they would be stranded when the
long winter set in. Finally, having failed, they packed
up their tent. When they were about to leave they
shouted abuse:

"I have travelled all over the world, including the
most primitive places and have had talks with the
chiefs of many tribes. I've failed too, but this time is beyond comprehension: the talks have gone on longer
than a marathon, without any result whatsoever!"

The couple shook hands with Gunsa, said their final
farewells and gave him some batteries. They had become good friends.

The residents of Luoda had skilfully used delay tactics and climatic conditions to win a victory. They had done every bit as well as their ancestors. So they organized a celebration on a scale that hadn't been seen for years. They struck their gongs and waved their torches in revelry, celebrating the departure of the foreign gods of pestilence.

Two months later, they learned that their celebrations had been a complete farce. A villager who had come to visit his relatives said a European couple carrying a baby had stayed in his village behind the mountain for several days. They were treated cordially and continued on towards Lhasa. It had been heard that officials from Lhasa had been dispatched to receive them. When the residents of Luoda heard this they were at a loss to explain how this obstinate couple had managed to get past them. For thousands of years they had been instructed to keep out intruders at any price. For this purpose their ancestors had paid with their lives.

The residents suddenly felt that they'd been sold out. Although they were extremely indignant there was nothing they could do and the town sunk into an atmosphere of loneliness and despair. Someone recalled that when the flying lama flew behind the mountain two large flowers fell from his stomach and floated down gradually. They were indeed heartbroken.

The day Gunsa left, he gave several balls of wool to Nganini and his radio to Yonna. She knew he was leaving for good. Man is reborn many times and she believed in another life she was destined to be with him. Although she wasn't sad, she couldn't bear to see him go. When they were about to part Venus had just appeared in the night sky and they said their last farewells under the walnut tree. She clutched the radio, not taking her eyes off him until he had vanished in the darkness.

Ten days later she inadvertently turned on the radio and listened to the news from a neighbouring country:

" .... After crossing the frontier, Prince Gunsa was met by border troops who carried out a brief and solemn welcoming ceremony. Government and military officials escorted him to the Amulazhuoder station. He arrived safely in the capital yesterday afternoon. To date, the reason for his capitulation has not been revealed.

That ends the news. We invite you to stay tuned to our music show."

西藏: 系在皮绳扣上的魂

扎西达娃

熊猫丛书

*

中国文学出版社出版

(中国北京百万庄路 24 号)

中国国际图书贸易总公司发行

(中国北京车公庄西路 35 号)

北京邮政信箱第 399 号   邮政编码 100044

1992 第 1 版 (英)

ISBN 7−5071−0087−1/ I.81 (外)

00900

10 − E − 2765P